*Getting Started in*

# Financial
# Information

## The Getting Started in Series

# *Getting Started in*
# Financial
# Information

## Daniel Moreau
## Tracey Longo

John Wiley & Sons, Inc.

New York • Chichester • Weinheim • Brisbane • Singapore • Toronto

This book is printed on acid-free paper. ∞

Copyright © 2000 by Daniel Moreau and Tracey Longo. All rights reserved.

Published by John Wiley & Sons, Inc.

Published simultaneously in Canada.

This publication is designed to provide accurate and authoritative information in regard to the subject matter covered. It is sold with the understanding that the publisher is not engaged in rendering professional services. If professional advice or other expert assistance is required, the services of a competent professional person should be sought.

*Library of Congress Cataloging-in-Publication Data:*
Moreau, Daniel, 1949–
    Getting started in financial information / Daniel Moreau and
  Tracey Longo.
      p.  cm.—(Getting started in series)
    Includes index.
    ISBN 0-471-32429-9 (paper : alk. paper)
    1. Investments—Information services.  2. Investments—Information
  resources.  I. Longo, Tracey.  II. Title.  III. Series: Getting
  started in.
  HG4515.9.M67   2000
  332.6—dc21                      99-32352

Printed in the United States of America

10  9  8  7  6  5  4  3  2  1

# Contents

# Preface

If you're overwhelmed by the fast pace of the investment markets and mind-numbing breadth of investment information that's available today, you've come to the right place for help. In this book we've tried to lay out both the process of investing and the best of the information you can use as your investment tools. And we've tried to do it in the most user-friendly and informative format we could design. The goal is to help you sort through a myriad of information sources including newspapers, personal finance magazines, annual reports, mutual fund prospectuses, and news and web sites, and make the most of them.

By the time you've finished the book, you'll know how to:

✔ Find the types of investments that are best suited to your needs.

✔ Narrow the field of investments to those that have the best chance for long-term performance.

✔ Make the most of the one or two investment-related newspapers, newsletters, and magazines you need to peruse to find good investments and monitor their performance.

✔ Find the best online source of information, news, market data, and analysis for you.

✔ Sort through the growing number of online brokerage services, with an eye toward finding one that offers the best all-around services for the price.

Navigating the choppy investment waters can feel treacherous at times, especially if you're not experienced. But with the right information at your fingertips and the ability to pick investments you feel comfortable staying the course with, you'll soon discover that it's not so difficult getting started in financial information. It just takes some guidance, the right navigational tools and sage tips. Put them to use and you'll be able to build a portfolio that can see you through life.

# Acknowledgments

I would like to thank so many people involved in this book. First, Ted Miller, editor of *Kiplinger's Personal Finance Magazine*, where I spent many wonderful years. Doug Rogers of *Investor's Business Daily* who gave me the opportunity to learn so much about mutual funds. Deb Englander was kind enough to include me in this project. And finally, Tracey Longo, whose impact on this book is everywhere.

—DAVID MOREAU

I'd like to thank my editor Deb Englander and her assistant Olga Herrera Moya for having faith over the years and for being constant sources of information themselves. I'd also like to thank my family for putting up with a writer—let alone one who thinks she can follow the markets. That means you, Murph, Betty, Christopher, Jodi, and Dejan. And last I'd like to thank my best friend, my mom J.C., who taught me that family and friends are much more important than the juiciest story or the hottest stock tip.

—TRACEY LONGO

*Getting Started in*

# Financial
# Information

# Introduction

————————

**W**ho among us has missed the never-ending stream of news about the stocks that have made folks rich beyond their wildest dreams? A $1,000 investment in Dell Computer in 1988, the unrivaled performance leader of U.S. companies in the late 1990s, would be worth more than $350,000 today. The plucky computer company rewarded shrewd and lucky investors alike with a whopping 79% return over the past 10 years. And that's not chump change. No investor who put money in the stock market in the past decade can deny that it's been a fascinating ride. So much for the much-ballyhooed and cautionary historical stock market return of 12% you'll find cited in so many investment books. The stock market has been a runaway bull for a long time now, routinely handing in average annual returns of more than 20%. A 20% return can double your money in just four years. Have you jumped on for the ride? Or are you still sitting on the sidelines wondering how to take the first step toward a rewarding investment plan and a financially sound future?

Whether you think you have the makings of a flourishing do-it-yourself investor, want to make sure you maximize your 401(k) by picking decent mutual funds, or

1

know you need to double-check the work of your financial adviser to be prudent, being able to access the right information and ask the right questions is always vital to your investment success. This book is designed to help you do all of those things.

If you've been overwhelmed by the sheer volume of information out there you're definitely not alone, but that feeling of paralysis is about to dissipate. It's not that there aren't more sources of prediction, insight, and investment approaches than you should ever have to worry about. There are. And it's not that they can't be downright distracting or even misleading. They can. But that's precisely what makes finding the right information so challenging. Solid information gives you a fundamental understanding of what is happening and why. It also gives you the knowledge you need to discount a good deal of the noise and concentrate on those investments you believe will be beneficial.

That's where we come in. This book is designed to help you pinpoint and understand the crucial information you'll need to make informed investment decisions—including determining what kind of investor you are—without getting waylaid by the tons of breathy nightly news reports, wordy articles, and confusing data that gets thrown at you every day.

We'll start at ground zero—where every investment strategy should start—with you. We'll help you identify and capitalize on the strengths of your investing or would-be investing style while sidestepping some of your weaknesses, like sinking your money into some hot investment tip too quickly.

Mutual funds can be a great way for investors to begin investing—and an easy, effective way to build a solid and diversified portfolio that can last a lifetime. But with more than 4,000 funds to choose from, which ones should you select? Do you know how to find out a fund's style and determine whether it complements or duplicates your existing investments? Are the performance numbers in the newspaper enough to go on, or do you need a more complete picture of a fund's performance? We'll show you how to access one-, three-, and five-year returns quickly and painlessly, so you'll avoid putting your money in overnight success stories that fall off the charts tomorrow. You'll also learn how to get risk information on the funds you're interested in, so you'll be able to assess how well they'll perform when the stock market is booming and when it stumbles. And finally, you'll learn how to access expense information. Keep an eye on expenses and you'll be able to maximize your investment results over time. After all, a mutual fund that costs just 1% more a year to own than other funds in its category can actually cost you hundreds of thousands of dollars over your investment horizon.

If you're interested in investing in individual stocks, this book will show you how to access the right research so you can measure and understand a stock's performance and decide whether it's a good investment vehicle for you. You'll also get the information you need to determine if stocks on your buy list have beaten, kept pace with, or lagged behind the performance of their peers.

Think your portfolio needs a few bonds? What kind and how much? We'll give you the information you need to figure out which type of bonds will work for you, what interest rate they're paying, and their dates of maturity. You'll also learn how to get a bond's rating and how to determine how much risk you're taking when you buy a bond.

Buying investments is one of the most important steps you can take toward a sound financial future, but it's not the end of the story. You'll want to be able to monitor your investments. We'll show you where to turn for solid analysis and measurements of your fund's success and how well competing investments are doing, so you'll get a true sense of whether it's time to hold or fold.

Before you know it, you'll be thinking like an investor. You'll be able to skim investment magazines with an eye toward finding those industries, companies, mutual funds, or bonds you believe are worth tracking. You'll be able to use the morning newspaper to check your own investments, to see if they're being rocked by short-term dips in the market or holding their own against peers. If you're computer literate, you'll have no trouble searching the Internet for more information about a company or a list of the best mutual fund performers that invest in any particular sector of the United States or international economies. You might even get the chance to pooh-pooh the opinion of some talking head on one of the financial television shows, since you may have developed a better understanding of why the market has taken a nosedive or why technology stocks are soaring again. And if you work with a financial planner or adviser, you'll be armed with the right questions the next time he or she calls touting some must-have investment or tries to downplay the rotten performance he or she racked up in your portfolio.

In short, you'll be able to find out what investments (and advisers) can and can't do for you, how well they are and aren't performing, and how much they're costing you.

By the time you're finished with this book, you'll know how to make sense of the facts and the numbers— whether it's performance data or risk measurements. You'll be able to avoid getting bogged down in mind-numbing jargon and go right for the most important data you need. Whether you're most comfortable mining the newspapers and magazines, scouring the library, or surfing the Internet, we'll tell you where to look to get the information you need to invest wisely. When you do that, you transform pertinent information into the kind of knowledge you can harness to put your money to work for you for a lifetime.

# 1

# Why You Need Relevant Investment Information

When you're deciding where to invest your hard-earned money, your most valuable tool is information. People who create and grow their wealth in the market look for investment information from a variety of sources. It's not brain surgery, but like most worthy pursuits, it's not as simple as it looks, either. If it were, we could all just pick the stock or mutual fund that's been doing really well for the past year. Since past performance is no guarantee of future results when you invest, you really need to know the who, what, where, when, and why of an investment before you put your check in the mail.

It's your money, after all, which is why it's so important that the information you use to make a decision is accurate, timely, and concise. In fact, with Internet trading growing more widespread every day, instant information has become the norm. The problem is that there's just so much of it. How do you know what information to take in and what to ignore? To make things more interesting, some professionals, like Thomas Greeves, a Bethesda, Maryland–based financial planner, maintain that the decades-old rules of the investing game—such as buy low, sell high, and you'll make money—are changing. "I know people who have been waiting five years to buy some of the better technology stocks because they think they're not priced low

**performance**
how much
money an invest-
ment earns or
loses in interest
and dividends
combined. Perfor-
mance is a mea-
sure of how well,
or poorly, your
investment is
doing.

**risk**
how much
money a certain
investment can
lose. Risk is usu-
ally measured as
a percentage of
your investment.
To give clients an
idea of how
much they may
lose investing in
stocks, many
financial planners
cite 30% as a
level of risk.

enough," Greeves says. "They'll be waiting forever." In the meantime, investors like Greeves have cashed in on some so-called overvalued stocks—turning the shares of companies like America Online (which he bought for $22) into the workhorses of their portfolios (as we went to print, America Online stock was valued at $100 a share).

That's why good information has to be relevant and thoughtful and why you have to be in the driver's seat when it comes to using the information. After all, a hot Internet stock might have seemed like the best thing since sliced bread last year, but not if it's overtaken by a competitor, its price tumbles by 50%, and you need the money to buy a house or to pay a tuition bill in the fall. On the other hand, an Internet stock, or a mutual fund that invests in Internet stocks, might be a fine place for a portion of your long-term investments, your retirement plan, or your individual retirement account (IRA). Problem is, there are hundreds of Internet stocks and a growing number of Internet mutual funds. How do you compare them and how do you zero in on the ones that best suit your needs, tastes, and investment horizon?

Investments are not one-size-fits-all. They can have very different potential for *performance* and *risk*.

A stock is not just a stock; it's a culmination of everything a company is and produces as well as investors' perceptions of what it is and produces. For instance, online giant America Online soared more than 580% in 1998 while bread maker Sunbeam Corporation stumbled, losing investors 83% in the same 12-month period. Obviously, not all stocks are alike. So how do you find those investments that will work best for the money you want to sock away for your goals? How, at the end of the day, without having to get a Ph.D. in investing, do you find the kind of relevant information you need to make sound decisions?

## THE FUTURE IS RIGHT AROUND THE CORNER

At no time in history has relevant financial information and intelligence been more crucial than it is today as some 76 million baby boomers move toward retirement age and confront their need to plan and invest. Behind them stand younger generations of Americans, computer-savvy, Internet-aware, and financially oriented. The younger among us already grasp the value of socking away substantial amounts of money for their retirement—and do just that. Their motivation? They really believe that their personal savings will be their most important source of retirement income. As importantly, they know how to get the information they need quickly, right from the comfort and convenience of their computer, whether it happens to be at home or in the office. In short, they get the information from the Internet. It's not surprising, then, that in survey after survey they say they are confident that their investment activities will provide them with a comfortable retirement. They've realized the profound truth of *compound interest.*

**compound interest**
interest earned when you reinvest previously earned interest from your investments. By letting your earnings ride, you begin to earn interest on your interest.

It works like this: If as a 30-year-old you start tucking away even $20 a week—the cost of about six gourmet *caffè lattes*—in a mutual fund or stock that pays a not-unrealistic 10% average annual return, you'll have a nest egg worth over $260,000 35 years from now. Of course, as your income increases and you pay down college loans and other debt, the money you'll be able to put to work in investments will increase, too. The lesson for all of us is that you don't have to be rich to make money; you just have to be diligent and find some decent investments—which all starts with the right information.

Together baby boomers, Generation Xers, and those edging toward retirement or already in it are pumping trillions of dollars into the financial markets. Regardless of which group you're in, if you're investing, you fueled much of the phenomenal rise in the U.S. stock market in the 1990s. In effect, millions of us have become would-be Wall Street players, whether we know what terms such as *volatility* mean or not.

**volatility**
how much an investment is likely to fluctuate (increase and decrease) in value. Volatility is based on historical ups and downs, as well as how similar investments have performed.

## IF YOU DON'T PLAY, YOU CAN'T WIN

We're investing in droves because we can and because we must. We know the past decade has produced scores of real-life investment success stories. A onetime initial investment of $10,000 put into the Vanguard Index Fund on January 1, 1988, would have grown to $47,099 by December 1998. A $10,000 investment socked away in financial services juggernaut Charles Schwab Corporation in 1988, with its 10-year track record of 63.5%, would be worth $635,000 today. That's the beauty of compound interest, which allows you to earn interest on your interest, and so on and so forth. As you'll see for yourself, compound interest can really produce impressive results over time.

But while thousands of people retire comfortably each year—by using the knowledge they acquire to decide what investments will best serve their needs and by investing regularly in those vehicles—not everyone secures financial independence in their so-called golden years. Some don't invest or even save—and they pay the price. Cold hard fact: A whopping 25% of current retirees have a retirement that has fallen short of their expectations, according to the Employee Benefit Research Institute (EBRI), a nonprofit think tank in Washington, DC, that studies Americans' retirement and investment habits. In fact, a significant 20% of current retirees report that their standard of living is worse than they anticipated it would be in retirement. About 42% of current retirees don't think they'll be able to pay for long-term care, 22% worry they won't be able to cover medical expenses, and another 29% doubt they'll have enough money to travel or pay for the recreation or entertainment they had hoped for.

That's not so surprising when you consider that almost half of those who are currently retired say that Social Security payments are their most important source of income. Without a good bit of social engineering on the part of our politicians, future retirees probably won't find that Social Security is able to make payments large enough for them to survive on. The sad news is that there really are still people out there, a small percentage of mostly middle-aged, middle-class individuals, who believe that they will be able to depend on Social Security for the main chunk of their retirement income in the next quarter century and beyond. If you're thinking, "Fat chance," you're on the right track. Marilyn Bergen, president of Capital Management Consulting, a financial planning firm in Portland, Oregon, says that while she usually counsels investors to wait until age $59^1/_2$ to start tapping their retirement plan, she makes an exception for Social Security benefits. "The first time you can start taking a nickel from Social Security, take it," Bergen says. "Obviously we have our doubts it will be there for future generations."

The moral of the story is that it's better to invest a little bit more than you'll need to ensure financial independence than it is to tuck away little or nothing. And that's exactly what those retirees who have a poorer lifestyle than they anticipated did—invested little or nothing.

## BUILDING CONFIDENCE

How important is vital investment information? It seems the more Americans realize that they need to invest some of their own money to retire comfortably, the more they discover they don't know about investing. Is the glass half empty or half full? While 72% of Americans have saved something for retirement, that means that 28% haven't saved dime one, EBRI has found. It's also interesting to note that workers' confidence in their own financial preparations and prowess has dropped, even in the face of the longest-running *bull market* in history, and with all the readily available information floating around out there.

 **bull market**
a market in which investments and prices are increasing, as opposed to a bear market, in which investments and prices are declining.

To get to the heart of the matter, EBRI asked American workers how confident they were in their investment prowess (see Table 1.1).

The good news is that more people, just like you, are taking matters into their own hands. They realize that it's never too early or late to start learning about investing so they can put their money to work. Of course, everyone knows what a struggle finding the money to save and invest can sometimes be. Some of you are embarking on new careers, starting your own business, or even going back to school. Some of you have been diligent savers all your lives, but not necessarily savvy investors. Others are

| TABLE 1.1  How Confident Are You in Your Investment Skills? | | |
|---|---|---|
| Confidence Level | 1997 | 1998 |
| Very confident that I am doing a good job | 33% | 25% |
| Somewhat confident | 44% | 47% |
| Not confident | 23% | 28% |

Source: Employee Benefit Research Institute, Washington, DC.

late bloomers who may still enjoy living from day to day, but have started thinking about investing for a variety of reasons.

Why invest now? Some people are prompted to take the first step when they see the shaky efforts of their elders who attempt to retire. After all, fear can be a powerful motivator. Some people are concerned that their own time and opportunities are slipping by. Still others have watched neighbors and coworkers invest their money successfully and want to put their own money to work. Maybe you've accumulated a tidy nest egg in your retirement plan at work and now want to do the same in a nonretirement account. Regardless of which camp you're in, you'll benefit from the kind of straightforward investment information that encourages intelligent decision making.

## JUMP ON THE BANDWAGON

It's heartening to discover that as a nation we in the United States are getting smarter about our need to save and invest. The number of people who have attempted to figure out how much they'll need to save by retirement is also increasing. Already almost half of baby boomers, who are recognizing the fact that they may spend 20 or more years in retirement, have attempted to calculate their own future financial needs themselves, EBRI has found (see Table 1.2).

There's more good news where that came from. We

| TABLE 1.2  Who's Trying to Determine How Much They'll Need to Retire? | | | | |
|---|---|---|---|---|
| Year | Preretirees | Older Boomers | Younger Boomers | Generation Xers |
| 1998 | 45% | 50% | 47% | 33% |
| 1997 | 44% | 38% | 32% | 30% |

*Source:* Employee Benefit Research Institute, Washington, DC.

have access to investment vehicles our ancestors just didn't have. The rise of the 401(k) plan in the 1980s, and its growing role as the primary retirement savings vehicle for workers across the country, has given millions of individuals the impetus they need to try to understand Wall Street and how it impacts their own personal finances.

No longer will millions count on company pensions and Social Security checks to fund their retirement years. They're making decisions now about how to invest their 401(k)s, their individual retirement accounts (IRAs), and their regular investments. By doing so, they're actually deciding how much they'll have to live on today, tomorrow, and down the road into retirement.

## SO MUCH TO CHOOSE FROM

Serving all of us eager investors is a burgeoning mutual fund industry, which already offers more than 7,000 funds and adds another 500 funds for investors to choose from each and every year. All told, in the United States some 66 million people have poured more than $5 trillion in hard-earned cash into their mutual fund accounts.

Stock pickers weren't left out of this investment explosion, either. A sea change in technology and a booming economy created thousands of initial public offerings (IPOs) of stock in the 1990s that boosted by some 2,000 the number of companies that are traded on the major stock exchanges. Now you can choose to invest in the stocks of more than 11,000 domestic companies. More than 60 million Americans do just that.

Companies and municipalities also gave investors a large offering of bonds to choose from. Not interested in individual bond investments? Look for one of the thousands of mutual funds that invest in different types of bonds.

## WHERE WE GET THE SCOOP

So where do people turn when trying to decide where to put their hard-earned dollars? (See Table 1.3.) Newspapers lead the way. The ever-growing financial press includes the *Wall Street Journal*, the *Financial Times*, *Investor's Business Daily*, and maybe even your local newspaper if it covers personal finance topics.

Newer magazines like *Individual Investor*, *SmartMoney,* and *Worth* have joined old-line publications like *Money* and *Business Week* to spread the word about decent stock, bond, and mutual fund offerings. Television programs such as *Wall Street Week* and the *Nightly Business Report* vie with CNBC and CNNfn to be the first to explain market changes and new investment opportunities to you. Morningstar, Value Line, and other analytical services that focus on mutual funds and their performance are moving to provide more news, analysis, and portfolio-tracking services than ever before. Financial news is now an integral part of almost every news broadcast.

| TABLE 1.3  Where Consumers Turn for Investment Information | |
| --- | --- |
| Newspapers | 78% |
| Television | 47% |
| Investment magazines | 44% |
| Recommendations from friends or relatives | 35% |
| Internet | 31% |
| *Source:* Dow Jones Newswires; J. D. Power & Associates. | |

Your financial library and local bookstores shouldn't be ignored, either. They bulge with dozens of well-written books on investing, saving for retirement, and understanding how to keep your home and family financially secure. Investment clubs that open up membership to mom, pop, and even kid investors have grown in number and attractiveness in the past decade. Despite the less-than-market-beating investment results of the best-known investment club in the country, the Beardstown Ladies', thousands of other investment clubs are delivering solid returns as a result of the real-money decisions members make based on their own investment research. As for the recommendations of friends and neighbors, well, as you can see from the table, lots of people use the thoughts and ideas of those around them as a basis for making investment decisions. If you're interested in the investments being suggested, however, take the time actually to see if the investments are worthwhile or just another stock or mutual fund that doesn't benefit your investment strategy or *portfolio*.

## INFORMATION CENTRAL

And then there is the Internet. It's clear even now while it's still in its infancy that the Internet has democratized investing by giving every Dick and Jane who's interested access to company and investment information that not so long ago only professional money managers were privy to. For those of you who have caught the wave, you know the Internet has profoundly heightened your ability to do financial planning by giving you access to vital data, information, and even useful calculators that can tell you nifty things like how much you need to invest at what interest rate and over what period of time to rack up a $1 million portfolio.

 **portfolio**
a collection of investments owned by an individual investor or a company, including certificates of deposit, stocks, bonds, and mutual funds.

## INVEST—NOW

We also have the ability, with the online trading services that many brokerage firms now offer, to act on our investment decisions almost instantly. Online trading may make the act of investing easier, but some critics allege that it presents huge risks to individual investors for that very same reason—because it makes investing so very fast and easy. Critics contend that as a result too many people will jump the gun and buy or sell stocks, bonds, and mutual funds without doing adequate research. Of course, if you're following the advice in this book you'll be able to tell those critics that you've already done your homework on the investments you buy and sell, and that online trading is just a tool you use to take some of the unnecessary paperwork out of buying and selling.

That's because in the proper hands the Internet can give you more information than you've ever had before to make decisions. For boomers wondering how much money they'll need to retire, how small company mutual funds are performing, or what Treasury bonds are paying, the answers are only a few computer keyboard strokes away. Those answers should make you a more—not less—thoughtful, competitive investor.

We're a long way from the days when a mainframe computer took up the whole office. There is growing evidence today that tells us that the Internet will become the principal way that in the not-so-distant future many people do the bulk of their financial research, if not their actual investing. Banks, brokerage firms, insurance companies, and mutual funds have all invested millions in their Internet sites to ensure that we find the investments and services we are seeking quickly. Of course, how you invest is incidental. There are many very successful investors who don't use a computer to find their next stock or mutual fund. The phone and U.S. mail work just fine for them, and if you're sick of hearing about all this computer stuff, they can work fine for you, too.

The downside of all of this information is the potential for overload. Search for a decent growth mutual fund that invests in U.S. stocks, and you'll find 500 that appear to do the trick. Do you know what questions to ask to narrow down the competition until you find the right fund or funds for your goals? Some mutual fund managers are downright aggressive, buying and selling stocks every day. Others are satisfied to hold on to the stocks or bonds they already have and earn smaller profits, if they don't have to take on too much risk. All those mutual funds that look alike may in fact be very different when you scratch the surface.

Whether you're searching through hard copies of newspapers and magazines or doing your investigating on-line, with so much information at your fingertips finding the right facts can be a daunting task if you don't know what you're looking for or how to qualify the investments your search turns up. In the past, finding relevant answers used to mean a simple hunt at the library, or a visit to your broker's office to review an analyst's reports. Today, you can sit in your pj's if you want to and use your computer to sort through a jungle of information to find what's relevant (and what isn't) to your investment decisions.

## DON'T BELIEVE EVERYTHING YOU READ

Of course, as choices loom, so do fool's gold and investment scams—those so-called investment opportunities that sound too good to be true precisely because they are. Without accurate information, it's easier to fall prey to scam artists, especially those that operate online, providing investors with hot tips in e-mail and chat rooms.

The Securities and Exchange Commission (SEC), which regulates the U.S. stock market and many of those who issue and sell stock, has accused more than 23 different companies and individuals of using the Internet to commit fraud, often by acting as independent, unbiased sources of information when in fact most were getting paid by the companies issuing the stock, which was often worth just pennies. Other online scam artists have been caught attempting to induce a large number of unsuspecting investors to buy the stock they're touting so that there will be a price run-up that will allow them to sell their shares for a hefty profit. Unfortunately, as the owners of large chunks of a penny stock sell, the price of such stock usually tumbles, leaving unfortunate investors with just pennies on their dollars or, worse, nothing at all. By educating yourself and asking the right questions, you'll be able to steer away from these kinds of money-losing deals and toward legitimate investments.

## IN CONTROL

When you have the facts, you're in control. Sure, it takes some time and effort to do your own research. But there is concrete evidence that investment education has a measurable and positive impact on individuals' savings habits and behavior. People who seek out financial education or get it at work are much more likely to figure out how much money they'll need to finance a sound retirement and much more likely to invest to get there. That's what the rest of this book is aimed at doing: turning you into an inquisitive and skeptical researcher so you can ask the right questions and find the right answers on your journey to becoming a successful investor.

*Chapter*

## 2

# Good Investing
# Starts at Home

———————

S ometimes solid investing can seem more like an odyssey than the art and science it really is. One sets out for uncharted territory hoping to find, well, what? The greatest stock ever known to man- or womankind? How about an investment that meets our goals? Not our neighbor's goals or our workmate's goals, mind you, but our own. That should narrow the field quite a bit.

In short, to become a solid investor you need to set your goals and steer toward them, using all of the tools at your disposal. As you already know, the right information is your greatest tool. You need the full picture when you're investing. Anything less than that can be harmful. Part of developing that full picture means you have to know yourself, what you want, when you want or need it, and what you're willing to risk in the process for a chance at gain. Sound like an overwhelming dose of common sense? "It's not," says Evan Simonoff, the longtime editor of *Financial Planning* magazine in New York City. "Only you know when you'll need your money, how much you want to earn, and how much you can afford to lose." This know-thyself exercise is one of the most important steps you will take toward developing an *investment strategy*.

**investment
strategy**
a plan for investing that meets criteria such as your goals, time horizon, and tolerance for risk.

## YOUR STRATEGY

The greatest thing about a sound investment strategy is it will keep you on the straight and narrow—focused on where you want to go and on monitoring whether you're getting there. Are you achieving your goals or aren't you? And if you're not, what do you need to change to get back on track? Do you need to buy or sell a certain type of investment, rejigger those investments that you have, or change how much you're investing?

A clear strategy will also help stop you from making unnecessary mistakes and taking needless chances, says Simonoff. With your own goals firmly in front of you, you'll develop a master radar system for finding and tracking those investments that are suited to your goals. That system will also act as a filter, sorting the barrage of information we're all bombarded with daily so that only what is pertinent to your investment strategy gets through.

## WHAT DO YOU WANT?

This process starts with what you want out of life. (How often does someone ask you that?) What do you want? Now's your chance to decide. Determine what it is, deep down, that you really want. Work it through on paper, writing down your short-term, mid-term, and long-term goals, so you can see them there in black and white. Keep it handy, because you'll need it again in a minute.

Are there any surprises? Something that came bubbling up that you didn't even know was there or had forgotten about? We all have different goals, which makes life so interesting. Some people want to travel. Others hope to buy a house. Still others want to start their own business or go back to school. Maybe you're hankering for an A-frame in the mountains or the latest model Mercedes-Benz. "After you've had a chance to really think about your goals, decide which ones are serious and admit which ones are just wistful fantasy (the boat that would be fun to have, but a pain to keep up and a huge money drain)," say Marc Eisenson, Gerri Detweiler, and Nancy Castleman in their book *Invest in Yourself* (John Wiley & Sons, 1998). Or, if you refuse to give up your whims—and some of the greatest accomplishments are achieved by those who won't relinquish the so-called pipe dreams they have—at least be prepared to put a price tag on them and invest in earnest toward them.

Don't forget to throw in those things you know are inevitable, as well, even if you don't particularly want to think of them as goals or dreams right now.

## THOSE MUST-HAVES

For instance, retirement has to go on your list. But you probably already know that, since there is a very close correlation between those who want to retire well and those who begin an investment plan (that means you). Be sure to include those other "to do" items, as well, like sending your kids to college. However painful some of these items might seem, the fact that you've committed them to paper is a major step forward. In sight, in mind, to put a new twist on an old phrase. And how much nicer to be prepared than to have to scramble and make do in the face of some of life's defining moments. Do you really want to have to work until you're 85? If you do want to work, go for it, but make sure that you're in the position to call the shots by taking the steps to plan ahead now. Have you covered all your bases?

How can you make these goals, some of them years or even decades off, seem real? Visualize what you want. Tack pictures up on your refrigerator and inside your medicine cabinet, or put them in your wallet. Having a hard time visualizing what retirement looks like? Dream big. Cut out the photo of the beach house, the golf course, or the exotic locale that excites you. If working with children or the elderly is your preference, find photos or pictures that remind you of how nice it will be to have the leisure time and the independence to make your dreams come true. These visuals will be your motivators in your quest for information that is useful to your investment strategy.

## NOW FOR THE REALITY

You have your goals straight now, but do you know how much they'll cost? Be realistic. If it's a car, look in the newspaper for the market price. The same goes for a house. As for retirement, financial planners estimate that you'll need 60% to 75% of your current income to live comfortably in retirement. So, if you make $50,000 now, you'll need to have between $30,000 and $37,500 to live comfortably in retirement, provided of course you get your other ducks in a row. Wracking up huge amounts of debt along the way, for instance, might require you to have access to more than 75% of your current income in retirement.

That gives you an idea of what your goals and dreams would cost in today's dollars. Unfortunately, it doesn't take into consideration *inflation,* which has an erosive impact on how far your dollars will stretch in the future.

**inflation**
the rate at which prices on goods and services will increase each year, reducing the purchasing power of today's dollar in the future.

You can figure out how much further your retirement dollars will have to go or what the costs of your other dreams will amount to as a result of inflation by first determining how many years you have until you plan to achieve your goal and then using the inflation factor (from Table 2.1) that corresponds. To determine the factor, we've used an average 3% inflation rate over time.

If you have 15 years until you want to retire and you're aiming at having 75% of your current income (which is now $40,000 a year) to live on, here is how the math works:

| | |
|---|---|
| Annual income: | $40,000 |
| Percentage you'll need in retirement: | × 75% |
| What you'll need in today's dollars: | $30,000 |

| TABLE 2.1 Number of Years Until You Retire | |
|---|---|
| Until Retirement/Goals | Inflation Factor |
| 5 | 1.16% |
| 10 | 1.34% |
| 15 | 1.56% |
| 20 | 1.81% |
| 25 | 2.09% |
| 30 | 2.43% |
| 35 | 2.81% |
| 40 | 3.26% |

| | |
|---|---|
| Inflation factor if you have 15 years until retirement: | × 1.56% |
| Projected annual income you'll need in retirement: | $46,800 |

## IS TIME ON YOUR SIDE?

The number of years you are giving yourself until you want to (or have to) achieve your goals is very important. On the sheet where you listed your long-, mid-, and short-term goals, jot down when, in years, you expect to achieve each of these goals. The number of years you're giving yourself to meet each of your dreams lets you know what the impact of inflation will be on the purchasing power of your savings and investments. To be on the safe side, do the math using the inflation factors in the table to arrive at the inflationary costs of each of your goals. Now jot down the cost after inflation for each. It may not be romantic to think about how much inflation will gobble up the money you've earmarked for that romantic dream vacation to Bali in five years, but planning an investment strategy without realistic projections is like setting off on a road trip to the Grand

Canyon without any gas in the tank. Unless you live in a tent a few miles away from the precipice of one of the world's greatest wonders, you're not going to get there on fumes alone.

Think about time and when, in terms of years from now, you expect to achieve your goals. Knowing how long you have to save gives you a concrete idea of how much you need sock away to live it up, remodel that kitchen, or retire comfortably.

## HOW MUCH IS ENOUGH?

With a bit of deduction, how long you're giving yourself to achieve your goals tells you another must-know bit of information: how much you'll need to sock away at various interest rates to hit your mark. On average, investing in the stock market will earn you 10% to 12% a year. But remember that although the *average* annual returns range from 10% to 12%, in actuality, as you know if you have started tracking the average annual returns on several specific mutual funds, stocks, or bonds, performance can vary wildly depending on the economy as a whole, what types of industries are prospering and which are not, and whether the individual company you're following is run well. After all, the economy can be booming, an industry can be hot, and a stock can still fare poorly, either because of poor management or investor perception that the company is fighting an uphill battle or caught in a downhill spiral.

So how much do you need to save or invest to meet your goals? Check out one of the online investment calculators that allow you determine what you need to put away each month to achieve your dreams or at least meet your needs. For instance, www.Bloomberg.com offers a helpful calculator in its "Investing" site, which allows you to calculate your long-term savings in two ways: By plugging in the amount you want to save, the interest rate you hope to earn, and the amount of time you're going to let your investments ride, you can have the calculator tell you exactly how much you'll accumulate. The beneficial little device also lets you plug in your desired investment goal in dollars, your time horizon, and the interest rate you hope to earn and calculates how much you need to save monthly to hit your goal.

A good rule of thumb? The more time you have to invest, the less you'll need to invest every month to achieve your goals, providing returns stay fairly true to their averages. Here's what we mean: If you're 25 years old aiming to retire at 50 with $1 million, you'd have to invest $847 a month and earn an average annual return of 10% to hit your mark. If you're 50 aiming to retire at 65 (and note you have 10 years fewer to invest in the second example than in the first), it will cost you $2,662 each month.

## OVER TIME

How much your money earns over time can make or break your investment strategy. That doesn't mean you risk every cent you have on one stock bet. But, depending on your age, it may mean that you want to put a significant portion of your assets into a varied stock market portfolio using stocks, mutual funds, or both. That means steering clear of putting too much of your money in bonds, bond mutual funds, or really safe investments such as bank certificates of deposit (CDs). No, neither of us are brokers trying to sell you something. We're journalists. But we want you to know that playing it overly safe with the majority of your money can cost you a bundle over the years. Sock your money away in low-paying vehicles like CDs or money markets only if it's earmarked for short-term (less than five years) goals or the emergency savings part of your investment strategy. As an example of how much your actual savings will be worth over different time periods at varying interest rates, take a look at the numbers in Table 2.2, which show how much (or little) you earn if you save $100 a month.

| TABLE 2.2    Is Your Money Working for You? | | | | | |
|---|---|---|---|---|---|
| Return | 5 Years | 10 Years | 15 Years | 20 Years | 30 Years |
| 0% | $6,000 | $12,000 | $18,000 | $24,000 | $36,000 |
| 5% | $6,829 | $15,592 | $26,840 | $41,275 | $83,573 |
| 8% | $7,397 | $18,418 | $34,835 | $59,294 | $150,030 |
| 10% | $7,808 | $20,655 | $41,799 | $76,570 | $227,936 |
| 12% | $8,247 | $23,334 | $50,457 | $99,915 | $352,992 |

Table 2.2 gives you an idea about how crucial the interest you earn on your money becomes over the long term. Here's the unavoidable truth: You'll earn almost two times as much if you earn 8% and almost three times as much if you earn 10% as you'll grow at 5% over a 30-year investment period. Think about that if you're the type of person that finds it easier to let bank CDs roll over automatically or let checking account money remain interest-free than it is to find decent investments. No one will guarantee the interest rate or return you'll earn when you invest (except maybe banks that are paying 3% on CDs while they receive two to three times that much by investing your money for their coffers). But over the long term the odds are on your side that you'll outearn safe accounts.

Which brings us to the next subject: risk. There are some very simple questions you have to ask yourself as you build your investment strategy: How much *can* you lose? How much can you *stand* to lose? Are your eyes as big as your stomach? Make sure you have a clear understanding of what the potential for loss is for any type of investment. Table 2.3 shows you how well, decade-by-decade, different types of investments have fared.

As you can see, on average there are few instances where investors lost money when they were invested over a long period, such as 10 years. Investors sustained the greatest loss in an individual asset class of small company stock in the 1920s, where the stock category

| Investment | 1920s | 1930s | 1940s | 1950s | 1960s | 1970s | 1980s | 1990s |
|---|---|---|---|---|---|---|---|---|
| **TABLE 2.3 Investors' Scorecard: Average Annual Performance of Types of Investments** | | | | | | | | |
| Large company stock | 19.2% | –0.1% | 9.2% | 19.4% | 7.8% | 5.9% | 17.5% | 17% |
| Small company stock | –4.5% | 1.4% | 20.7% | 16.9% | 15.5% | 11.5% | 15.8% | 16.5% |
| Long-term corporate bonds | 5.2% | 6.9% | 2.7% | 1.0% | 1.7% | 6.2% | 13.0% | 10.8% |
| Long-term government bonds | 5% | 4.9% | 3.2% | –0.1% | 1.4% | 5.5% | 12.6% | 11.3% |
| Treasury bills | 3.7% | 0.6% | 0.4% | 1.9% | 3.5% | 7% | 11.9% | 8.3% |

on average lost –4.5%. Of course, as a wise investor once noted, you don't want to roll up your pants and stroll across the Potomac River based on the average depth. What that means is if you were invested in a single small company stock during the 1920s, you could have lost a lot more, lost nothing at all, or even had a gain on your investment.

## BIG RETURNS, BIGGER RISKS

Before you invest, you should also take a look at how a particular investment has performed over time, so you'll be acclimated to what can happen long before it does happen. It also pays to realize that the greater the return or the potential for return, the greater the potential for loss. In other words, a stock that generally returns about 10% a year is less risky or volatile than one that returned 160% last year.

To comprehend the full weight of how average gains or losses may not be representative of what you actually gain or lose, let's look at some recent examples of how some well-known stocks have performed.

How do you think certain stocks fared in 1998? DuPont, the well-known rubber and synthetics corporation, lost a stinging –9.8% that year. But over three years the giant company had an average annual return of 17.6%, over five years it racked up a 20.2% return, and over 10 years it gave investors back a respectable 17.5%. Remember, a stock's past performance is absolutely no guarantee of what might happen to your money in the future. At the same time, as DuPont's 1998 performance makes obvious, today's performance is no guarantee of what a stock will do over time—good or bad.

## CAN YOU LIVE WITH RISK?

The question you must ask yourself before investing is this: Can you live with the potential for risk that you discover? In general, you should set parameters regarding how much you're willing and able to lose. Money you cannot afford to lose—such as any funds that are earmarked for a must-pay bill like tuition, the balloon payment on a mortgage, or a relative's long-term care—should not be put in the stock market. Alternately, without any risk, your earning potential is slim to poor, a notion that is spelled out more graphically in Table 2.2.

**interest income**
the interest your investments earn in any given year.

For years one of the more popular rules of investing has had investors subtracting their age from 100 to determine how much of their assets they should put in the stock market—for instance, 100 minus age 30 equals 70% in the stock market.

But that rule ignores your comfort level with risk and the fact that people are staying invested in the stock market later in life than ever before (especially those who can live off the *interest income* their investments generate without touching the *principal*).

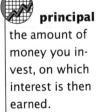

**principal**
the amount of money you invest, on which interest is then earned.

Financial planners usually use a 20% potential loss scenario to educate their clients about the real potential for investment loss. Could you live with that? The bottom line is that the longer you stay invested, the less you're likely to lose. Ibbotson, a Chicago-based research and consulting firm, crunched stock market returns for more than 80 years and discovered that an investor who is investing for a 10-year time period is likely to lose money only 3% of the time. If that same investor wants to stay invested for only five years, the chances of losing money increase to 10% of the time. The longer you're in, the less likely you are to lose.

## MINIMIZE YOUR RISK

Why is information so important to how and where you invest? Here's an example from real life. You're glancing through a magazine in your doctor's office and an item catches your eye touting the fact that a company is launching a new product that seems sure to take its competitors by storm. It's a no-lose proposition for professional photographers, the article says. But what does any of this mean to investors? Do you buy stock in the company?

Polaroid issued several new products in the past few years. But product alone is not the complete story for any corporation. Here's why: Despite those new products and a spiffy image, Polaroid's competitors, especially those in Asia, have been winning out with lower-priced offerings. The result? Polaroid's stock lost 60% in 1998.

Of course, if you had a portfolio of 20 different stocks, in theory some would perform well, some would do poorly, and some would be just average. The point, however, is that your portfolio's overall return should put you in the black. No one losing investment should be able to put you in the red.

This practice of spreading risk among a variety of companies, industries, mutual funds, and/or bonds is called *diversification*.

The trick is not to have too few investments or to go overboard. Don't load down your portfolio with any one

**diversification** a strategy of spreading your money out in an array of investments, which ideally move out-of-step with each other, in an attempt to protect your overall portfolio against a potential loss in any one investment.

stock—even if it's stock your company issues—or you'll take on an unnecessary concentration of risk. At the same time, it isn't wise to invest in too many investments, either. If you're investing $10,000, start out with no more than three or four investments (whether they're stocks or mutual funds), or you'll get overwhelmed. And never have so many investments your portfolio becomes unwieldy and difficult to monitor.

One of the most important rules of diversification is not to put all of your eggs in one basket. By one basket we mean one type of industry and any one sector of the economy. Concentration leads to unnecessary risk. An example of one basket investing would be the guy who puts all of his money in semiconductor stocks. Even putting all of your money in blue chip stocks may be a little risky. As you build your portfolio, keep an eye on which investments make up what portion of your portfolio, so you can ensure that no one stock, bond, mutual fund, or industry dominates.

Again, it doesn't have to be mysterious. Don't forget that sound investing starts with determining where you want to go with your investment strategy, how long you have to get there, what your performance expectations are, and what your risk tolerance is. These four pieces will shift and become more refined over time, and that's perfectly normal. The important part is that in defining these aspects of your financial life you're increasing the chances that you'll succeed as an investor.

### More Rules of the Investing Road

To help you reach your goals, here are a few more principles of investing you should understand before you do any research or invest a penny of your money. We're repeating a few rules of thumb, but some bear repeating and should be underpinnings of your investment approach.

• *Don't jump on the train when it's running out of track.* Stocks go up and down. Over the years different stocks come into favor as others go out of favor. While car stocks may be hot one year, a few years later they'll drop off the charts. If a certain sector of the stock market has been red-hot for several years, chances are you may have missed the ride. Instead of pouring too much money into this overheated sector, look for the next stock market sector that's likely to come into vogue. That's in keeping with that old, but steady mantra: Buy low, sell high.

• *Set parameters for buying and selling.* Don't buy just to buy or because neighbors or workmates are buying. Look at the price history of a stock or mutual fund, so you can watch it over time and make at least a stab at buying the investment at a price that gives you some value. Like buying a house that is overpriced, you may have to hold a significantly overpriced stock for years and years before you can sell at a profit. The same goes for selling. Keep focused on why you bought an investment in the first place. Sell when those *fundamentals* have changed or if, because of great returns, a stock has begun to dominate your portfolio and you feel that to manage risk you need to reduce your position.

• *Remember that if it sounds too good, it is.* Don't believe anything you read or hear about an investment without checking out the news yourself and evaluating it using the radar you'll start developing. There are many people who are making a living touting stocks on the Internet or over the phone. Even well-meaning brokers who earn their living by selling stocks may try to sell you something that's not promising or a good fit. Don't hesitate to put the brakes on if you have questions. Get your questions answered first. It's better to wait while you do your investigation than get duped.

**fundamentals**
the underlying, historical information on dividends, earnings, sales, and profits that can help you form a picture of a company's prospect for future success.

*(Continued)*

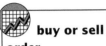

**buy or sell order**
an order you place either to buy or to sell bonds or shares of a stock.

• *Look for hidden costs.* No one works for free. Brokerage firms and mutual funds are all in business and they all charge fees. Brokerage charges for selling you a mutual fund may range as high as 5.75%, which can significantly eat into your returns. Commissions that brokers charge for taking a *buy or sell order* for a stock or bond can also burn up the investment's actual performance. At the same time many investments have internal costs—for instance, stock mutual funds charge investors about 1.5% annually, while annuities can cost you as much as 6% of your initial investment. While financial planners can help you figure out your investment strategy and select investments, they often tack on an additional 1% fee annually or may charge commissions for buying or selling investments for you.

• *Avoid paralysis and profound disappointment.* Remember, if something doesn't work the way you predicted it would, it's never too late to sell. Over your lifetime, you'll buy and sell a number of investments. It's also likely that as you invest and experience gains and losses, you'll grow a bit more tolerant of risk. Time, as professional money managers say, has a way of evening out highs and lows, end to end. What that means is that if you take a snapshot of a stock one day, it might be up or down significantly. But over one year, five years, or a score, the volatility will look far less, well, volatile.

• *Dollar cost average.* If you find a great investment at what you believe is a great price, buy it. If you're less apt to follow the markets day in and day out, the alternative is dollar cost averaging, which allows you to set up an automatic investing program that buys certain shares of a mutual fund or stock at regular intervals. You can add to your portfolio this way each month. The beauty of dollar cost averaging is that it evens out the highs and lows of an investment's performance and price over time.

• *Why am I investing?* That's the question every smart investor begins his or her investment plan or strategy with. The plan then outlines your investment goals, your time line, and the amount of money you will save and invest to reach your goals. The plan should be long-term, with a time horizon of at least five years. It is diversified among various investments like stocks, bonds, mutual funds, and cash, which you monitor at least annually.

• *Beat inflation.* The baseline reason to invest is of course to make money, but you also have to beat inflation, which averaged about 3% throughout the 1990s. If you can't beat inflation, you aren't really making money. Inflation is low now, but even 4% inflation, which for anyone who was an adult in the 1970s would seem minute, can be very corrosive, severely reducing the buying power of the money you're socking away for retirement if you don't put your money to work earning interest.

• *Get out the yardstick.* All investment performance is measured against some benchmark like the Standard & Poor's 500, or the interest rate paid by U.S. Treasury bonds or the rate of inflation. Benchmarks' performance represent the average performance of a fairly static group of investments. It's a fair assessment of how well you did in comparison to the average performance of like investments. Make sure, however, that you compare apples to apples. An index that measures U.S. stock performance is not a good performance benchmark for international stocks or mutual funds. Thanks to the raging bull market of the 1990s, index investing—which is often used to describe a

*(Continued)*

style of mutual fund that invests all of its funds in the stocks or bonds that make up a particular index or benchmark—has become very popular, often beating managers who actively buy and sell investments.

• *Keep in mind that risk and reward are closely linked.* That is, the greater reward you hope to earn or are earning, the greater the risk you're taking and the more you can hope to earn or expect to lose. Risk is everywhere in investing, even in holding cash, but it is manageable. Much risk is measurable using a variety of mathematical calculations.

• *Know your risk tolerance.* Every investor has a tolerance for risk. If you don't know yours, you can complete a simple quiz offered by most mutual fund companies and brokerages that will help you determine how much risk you should take. Sage (www.sage.com) has a good one you can take online. Risk management means learning activities that are essentially counterintuitive practices. Buying when the market is down rather than at its peak is one practice that runs counter to what feels most intuitive or seems most practical to us. But investors must learn these practices in order to maximize their investment dollars.

• *Be assured there's no mystery to investing.* As we'll explain in Chapter 4, all investment is either equity or debt. If you own equity, you own assets like shares of company stock or a mutual fund. If you're investing in debt, you own bonds or notes, which are agreements from a corporation to repay a loan. Money market mutual funds are debt, too. The money you deposit in a money market gets loaned to a corporation, which in turn pays you interest on the loan. Bank money market accounts and CDs are still other forms of debt.

## What Makes Investors Succeed

Who wins at investing? Oh, there will always be stories about the high school student who invests in a hot new stock and earns 900%. But that's more akin to beating the odds in Las Vegas or winning the lottery than it is to investing. Investors with a systematic and disciplined approach to investing who do their homework and research up front and stick to their techniques through a market's ups and downs tend to be the most successful. Such investors are not diverted by extraneous advice, dubious information, or get-rich-quick schemes. Instead they develop a base of knowledge and a cadre of investments—whether stocks or mutual funds—that they follow over time so they understand the nuances and their importance. They also don't trade—buy or sell—without sound reasons because they understand that there are costs associated with buying and selling (actual trading costs, brokerage commissions, and fees for cashing out of certain mutual funds and most annuities in the earlier years of the investment) that can severely eat up any performance your portfolio racks up.

*Chapter*

# 3

# The Basics of
# Being an Investor

For all investors, even long-term investors who have years in front of them to save for retirement, the reason to gather financial facts is fairly simple. We all want to buy investments that grow the fastest with the least amount of risk.

Say that rapidly and it sounds easy. And that is the mythical lure of investing: Make the right decisions and you're wealthy, sometimes overnight. If life were a movie about Wall Street, the drama might play out that way. But it's not and you don't have to make spur-of-the-moment decisions regarding your money. You also shouldn't expect to get rich overnight. It's precisely those investors who want to be part of a quick rags-to-riches story who are most likely to bet everything they have on some "sure winner" or get taken in by an investment scam or a bad brokers' offering that would seem too good to be true to the rest of us. That's not investing; it's gambling.

Sound investing means "we diversify and we set reasonable and realistic goals," says Matthew Reading, a partner with the financial planning firm of Austin Asset Management in Austin, Texas. "If a client's goal is 10% a year until retirement, and that's what they'll need to live very well, we don't need to take on the risk of trying to earn 50% in a year."

34

In reality, we know that wealth accumulates over time, the result of decisions that are based on careful analysis of sound information. In keeping with reality, however, we also know that we need to throw into the mix a willingness to take on some degree of calculated risk. But the most successful long-term investors are not speculators who bet the farm on a hunch or whim, but individuals with a solid understanding of their goals and what it will take to reach them, a heightened sense of opportunity, and a working knowledge of how business and investments work. They also have an investment strategy, as we discussed in Chapter 2. They know how to judge what to own, how to manage it, and how to monitor it to see if it is performing up to snuff.

"The best individual investors I've seen are those who stay on top of their game and know what to expect," says Dan Sondhelm, vice president of Morrison/Carlisle, Inc., in Alexandria, Virginia, a strategic financial relations firm that works with a number of mutual fund managers across the country. "They're not thrown by news about a company or an industry because they've already done their homework. They're not necessarily buying or selling investments all of the time, but they certainly know when opportunity knocks and when not to respond to shorter-term volatility."

You can be that kind of investor, too. It takes preparation. The preparation begins here with the fundamentals of investing. We'll start with what we mean when we say investments. Then we'll outline some straightforward principles that guide those who invest successfully. We'll show you what you can expect to learn in your research. And to help give you a sense of what kind of investor you are, we'll offer a half dozen or so profiles of investor types. After that careful preparation, we'll dig into the vast store of financial information that is available and show you the best places to look for the facts.

## WHAT ARE INVESTMENTS?

When we talk about investments, we mean stocks, bonds, mutual funds, and instruments such as certificates of deposit (CDs) that are commonly thought of as cash equivalents. Depending on your goals, you'll want to own some or all of these investments. To maximize your investment opportunities, you'll need to familiarize yourself with these terms and how these vehicles work.

## WHAT'S SO GREAT ABOUT MUTUAL FUNDS?

A mutual fund is an investment company that pools investor money to buy shares of stocks, bonds, or both. When you invest in a mutual fund, you purchase shares in the fund, which in turn owns shares in the underlying assets it invests in. If a fund invests part of its cash in IBM stock, you own a mutual fund that invests in IBM. You do not own IBM shares themselves directly. That's important to remember with mutual funds since IBM may take a beating, but because of the numerous other stocks or bonds your mutual fund holds, your fund may still perform quite well.

That's because mutual funds are diversified and cannot by law put all their eggs in one basket—one stock or one bond—though there are *sector funds* that invest in one segment of the economy, such as financial services, precious metals, real estate, or technology. While a sector mutual fund will be far more concentrated than an ordinary fund that buys an array of stocks from a number of different industries, a variety of bonds, or both, it still by law cannot put all its eggs in one stock or bond. For this reason, we say that mutual funds are diversified, investing in either a number of industries or entities or at least in a number of stocks or bonds. By spreading money around among a number of investments, mutual fund managers mitigate risk.

**sector funds**
mutual funds that specialize in a sector of the economy. For example, the stocks of banks, insurance companies, and brokerage firms would make up the portfolio of a financial services sector fund.

### Why They're Good for Beginners

You can invest in a number of very solid mutual funds for as little as $1,000. But even if you choose just one, you'll still be investing in 20 or more stocks and bonds because that's about the minimum number of investment bets that a mutual fund manager makes in any one fund portfolio.

That's very different from an individual investor putting his or her first $1,000 in one stock. With one stock, your fortune rests on the success or failure of one company. Investing in a minimum of 20 instruments (Janus 20, a great-performing mutual fund in the 1990s, is one of the few growth mutual funds that invests in only 20 stocks) means that one of a fund's stocks or bonds may fare extremely poorly and the overall mutual fund may nevertheless do very well because of its other investments. That's the beauty of mutual funds and why they're a good choice for beginning investors.

There are other reasons, as well, why choosing a mutual fund or several is a good choice for someone taking a first step as an investor. One of the greatest things about mutual funds is that for as little as a $1,000 investment—the minimum initial investment required by some very solid funds—you're buying professional money management. In the past, investors needed hundreds of thousands of dollars even to interest money managers in managing their accounts. In contrast today, every person who invests in a mutual fund gets a manager—or even a team of managers—who closely monitors the performance of the fund's individual investments minute-by-minute throughout the day, always with an eye toward finding the best stocks or bonds to buy and the weakest ones to sell.

Take, for instance, the high-flying world of technical stocks. Knowing enough about the industries represented in this sector, let alone about the individual companies and their products and managers, can be a tall order. Picking some of the newer tech stocks isn't like picking the best carmaker, says Kevin Landis, a mutual fund manager with Firsthand Funds. These are new industries creating new technologies and products where the demand can be virtually unknown. "But if I want dynamic growth I have to embrace or at least tolerate the idea there are some unknowns," says Landis, who argues that those who don't see themselves as dyed-in-the-wool stock pickers are better off in mutual funds letting money managers pick stocks for them.

Why are mutual fund managers so attentive to the little investors in their fund? Because your money is pooled with the money of other investors, which gives fund managers a large chunk of change to manage and far greater buying power than most individual investors (or some money managers, for that matter) would have on their own.

There really is power in numbers. Take a look at T. Rowe Price's Blue Chip Growth Fund, which racked up an outstanding 28.8% return in 1998. More than 150,000 people have invested more than $4 billion in this mutual fund over the past decade. That's a lot of money and to make sure no one stock made or broke the fund's performance, its manager invested in more than 40 stocks. While some of the companies the fund invested in lost money, the fund still managed to edge out the Standard & Poor's 28.5% return by owning some winning stocks.

Even if it seems like we're beating a dead horse, we'll say this again: Owning only one mutual fund is far less concentrated and hence of lower risk than owning one or even five stocks. The only exception to this rule of thumb that states that mutual funds are less risky than individual stocks are sector funds that invest in just one industry such as technology.

### What You'll Pay for Mutual Fund Shares

Like a company's stock, a mutual fund divvies up its investment pool into shares. When you buy a share, you're buying a piece of the fund's potential for gain and loss. A fund's share price reflects the fluctuating value of the underlying assets (stocks and/or bonds) it invests in. Fund shares are repriced daily to reflect the changes in these securities' prices. Prices for most mutual funds are published in all but the smallest daily newspapers, are available on each fund family's web site, and can be easily obtained by calling the fund family's toll-free phone number. There's no mystery there.

That's why mutual funds are the most popular investment vehicle for millions of individual investors. They allow you to get exposure to just about any type of investment market you want, whether it's small U.S. company stocks, international bonds, or even sector funds. You can get in and out of mutual funds relatively easily (though you should restrict active trading in mutual funds to minimize the taxes you'll pay on gains), and there is a sense that professional money managers will do a better job than you can at investing your money. By owning shares in a mutual fund, you are also relieved of the responsibility of deciding when to buy and sell individual stocks and bonds, which can quickly become a full-time job.

## Minimizing Your Risk

As we've mentioned, funds can be less risky because in a mutual fund your money is spread among numerous and different stocks or bonds instead of relying on any one or just a handful to make or break investment performance. Most investment professionals believe that it's wiser to own a variety of stocks and bond investments, rather than gamble on just a few. That's called diversifying your portfolio.

Spreading your risk (and money) among a variety of investments that behave in different ways during different market conditions is believed to reduce your risk of loss. To further diversify your risk, you'll want to build your investment portfolio with a mix of investments that are suitable to your goals, your age, and your tolerance for risk.

For example, technology funds are about 85% riskier than the S&P 500, according to a new report from Leah Modigliani, an investment strategist with Morgan Stanley Dean Witter, who suggests that the added risk shaves at least a few performance points off almost all tech mutual funds. The good news is that when used in a diversified portfolio, the volatility of tech funds drops to about 35% more risk than the S&P 500. There's the importance of diversification again.

While sector funds, such as a technology mutual fund with a decent performance track record, can be a good addition to an overall portfolio, don't make it your first mutual fund unless you can stand to see your fortunes bounce up and down—sometimes by as much as 20% to 30% in the course of just one day.

Here's a look at how diversification works in real life to minimize or maximize risk and performance (Table 3.1). You can see what your potential for gains and losses is over the long term, and also gauge your own risk com-

| TABLE 3.1    Matching Long-Term Goals to Your Risk Tolerance | | | |
|---|---|---|---|
| 1955–1998 | Lower Risk/ Return Portfolio | Moderate Risk/ Return Portfolio | Higher Risk/ Return Portfolio |
| | 20% stability: money markets | 10% stability: money markets | 20% income: bonds |
| | 40% income: bonds | 30% income: bonds | 80% growth: stocks |
| | 40% growth: stocks | 60% growth: stocks | |
| Return for best year | 22.8% | 28.1% | 35.0% |
| Return for worst year | –6.7% | –13.4% | 19.6% |
| Average annual return | 9.0% | 10.1% | 10.9% |
| Number of down years | 8 | 8 | 9 |
| Average loss in down years | –2.0% | –6.7% | –7.1% |

Source: T. Rowe Price Associates, Inc., Baltimore, MD.

fort level, by looking at how several long-term sample portfolios fared over the past 44 years.

There is risk attendant in investing in both stocks and bonds and in mutual funds. Since there are no performance guarantees, no one ensures that the principal you invest will be returned. As a result any stock or bond—or the overall market—can fare poorly. Of course, there is also the risk of human error since all companies and mutual funds are managed or at least steered by real, live humans. To reduce the risk of painful loss, invest only what you can afford to live without for five years or more. The reason why is that stocks and bonds—and as a result, the mutual funds that invest in them—go up and down due to market factors. If you will need to buy a car next year, you don't want your $20,000 to be down 20% when you have to have it in 12 months. Markets have always rebounded in the past, but you may not want to do without a car waiting for that to happen. Put money you need within five years in cash equivalents (money market mutual funds fall in this category) where you can earn some interest without risking your principal.

### I Can See Clearly Now

To understand risk more clearly it's important to understand that mutual funds fall into two basic categories: stock funds and bond funds. Each has different risks because fund portfolios can vary greatly, based on the stated objective of the mutual fund manager doing the managing. The *mutual fund objective* will give you an initial read of what a fund manager's goals are and whether they mesh with your own.

Fund managers attempt to select investments they believe will fulfill the stated objectives—whether growth, income, or both growth and income. Managers aiming for future growth may select only the smallest of companies that specialize in technology. That fund would be significantly riskier than a fund designed to provide steady income that invests mainly in U.S. Treasury and high-rated corporate bonds. For a more in-depth discussion on mutual fund investment objectives, see Chapter 4.

**mutual fund objective**
the stated investment objective of the mutual fund manager selecting the fund portfolio. The three most common objectives are: growth, income, or both growth and income.

### Stock Mutual Funds

Not surprisingly, these funds invest primarily in stocks. The question you'll need to ask, though, is, what kind of stocks? In other words, what kind of companies and industries is a fund manager betting will allow him or her to meet the stated objective?. There are as many different stock funds as the day is long. For instance, some funds buy only blue chip stocks because their objective is income and safety. Others may buy high-growth companies such as Internet product and service providers because they're willing to take on quite a bit more additional risk to emphasize future gains.

### The World, Your Oyster

Then there's the entire world, which includes *international, world, and global funds* you can pick and choose from.

**international, world, and global funds**
funds that invest in a portfolio of non-U.S. stocks and/or bonds. They may also, in the case of world and global funds, invest in the U.S. markets as well.

These funds almost exclusively aim for long-term or aggressive growth, which means somewhat more risk. But for a longer-term investment, such as one designated for retirement, international investments are a good way to diversify so that you're not putting all your eggs in the U.S. stock and bond market basket. Be careful what you choose, however, since international funds can concentrate their investments in one region of the world or even one country. Global or world funds also have the ability to concentrate much of their investments in the United States, which is fine as long as you're not buying the fund to *hedge* your exposure to the performance of the U.S. markets.

While international funds overall have the potential to produce some heady profits, they can also lose investors money if the countries or regions stumble. Funds that invested in Asian or even just Japanese companies in the 1990s gave investors some spectacular returns. But that came to a crashing halt in 1998, when the region's economy collapsed. When that happened, some of the funds' share prices fell as much as 60%. At the same time, however, some mutual funds that invested in European companies returned fine profits to their investors.

### Bond Mutual Funds

Bond funds can produce regular income like individual bonds do, but unlike bonds, bond mutual funds do not have a maturity date and they do not guarantee that the principal amount of cash you invest will be returned to you. So you can lose principal, as investors did in the late 1980s.

Like stock funds, bond funds vary greatly in terms of what they invest in. Look at the fund's objective for preliminary insight into what its manager is trying to accomplish. If a bond fund's stated objective is just plain income, it's likely the fund is investing in bonds with short-term and intermediate maturity dates, which create steady though only moderate income in return for a small risk of loss.

If a bond fund's objective is high current income, it's likely that the manager invests in high-yield bonds, also called *junk bonds*, whose issuers are in some danger of defaulting on their debt repayments—their bonds. Man-

**hedge**
to buy an investment that moves out-of-step with the rest of your portfolio, in order to diversify.

**junk bonds**
debt issued by those in some danger of defaulting on their debt repayments. Owning junk bonds can therefore be very risky.

agers use a variety of strategies to attempt to lessen risk. One routine strategy involves buying bonds with different maturity dates—short-term, intermediate, and long-term. That means that even if the bond market turns sour, it is likely that only a portion of the bonds will be impacted. Others will mature before or after the downturn occurs.

### *An Open or Shut Case*

Mutual funds are either open-end or closed-end. The value of open-end mutual fund shares—called *net asset value (NAV)*—is also the price that you can buy shares at. The NAV of a fund rises and falls based on the value of its overall holdings.

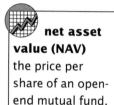

**net asset value (NAV)** the price per share of an open-end mutual fund.

Closed-end funds are an altogether different animal. Investors buy shares in the fund in an initial public offering. Once that offering is concluded, the fund is closed and shares are traded on a stock exchange like stocks, but often at a discount to the value of their underlying assets. That of course is no way to make money. Closed-end funds can trade at a premium to their initial offering price and thus provide a gain for investors. Emerging market closed-end funds, for example, rose in price and were hot properties in the early 1990s, but faded when the economies of many countries, including those in Eastern Europe and Latin America, took a nosedive toward the end of the millennium.

There are investors who buy closed-end mutual funds at a discount in the hope that their share prices will eventually rise to meet the value of the underlying assets. For most investors interested in the professional money management that mutual funds provide, however, a better choice is an investment in an open-end mutual fund, where one can buy and sell shares directly from and to a mutual fund company itself, or, for a commission, through a broker who will buy or sell the shares for you.

## THE LOWDOWN ON STOCKS

A stock is a share of equity in a company—in essence a piece of the corporate pie. When you own shares of stock

**dividends**
the portion of a company's profits paid out directly to its shareholders. A company's board of directors decides whether a company will declare and pay a dividend, and, if so, how large it will be.

**shareholders**
investors who buy shares when a company issues stock or ownership shares that it sells in the open or public market.

**leveraged**
having a large proportion of debt as opposed to capital.

you own a portion of the company. People who invest in a stock expect that the price of the stock will go up and that they may also earn *dividends*, if indeed the stock they buy pays them. If Company X declares a dividend of $5 per share and you own 1,000 shares, your dividend for the year is $5,000, which you can choose to be paid or to reinvest. Larger, older companies are more likely to pay dividends. Smaller ones usually reinvest profits to keep growing.

Companies issue stock as a way to raise money. They're willing to give up a fraction of control and undergo public scrutiny in exchange for raising capital to accomplish their strategic goals, whether that means expanding, taking over another company, buying equipment, or paying off debt.

When a company does well and it is perceived as successful by Wall Street analysts and investors, the stockholders, or *shareholders* as they are called, profit from the success.

When a company stumbles or its management blunders, the price of the stock can decline and shareholders can lose money. When they buy stock, shareholders take on the risk that the economy or the stock market overall might fare poorly or the company itself not prosper. That might happen because a company's managers, products, or services are faltering; the company doesn't have the ability to compete successfully; it is too *leveraged*; or the industry the company operates in is suffering a setback.

Lately, with a number of new investors entering the stock market for the first time, it has come to our attention that some investors believe that when the price of a share of stock declines they have lost money forever—as if someone stole money from a dresser drawer or their wallet—and it can never be retrieved. That isn't so. The price of stock fluctuates up and down over time. If the price of the stock you hold rebounds in a week, a month, or a year, you will be made whole and may even make a profit on the stock. To determine how much you have made or lost, obtain the share price and multiply by the number of shares you own. Say, for instance, the price of a share of Tracey's company is $80 a share today and you own 100 shares. Your shares are worth $8,000. If you paid more for the shares, you would've lost money if you sell them now. If you paid less, you've made money on the stock if you sell it now.

This is where your information sources can become crucial. When the price of a stock goes up or down significantly, you should be able to make an educated guess based on facts whether the price will rise or fall some more. You don't want to buy a stock when it's at its peak price. How can you earn a profit if you do? At the same time, if you think the price of a stock may rebound, you don't want to sell at its lowest price, either, because you'll take a loss you may be able to avoid by simply holding on to the shares for a period of time.

## Size Matters

There are three main categories of stock to consider: blue-chip (large-cap) stock, mid-cap stock, and small-cap stock. Size makes a difference since it influences a number of different investment factors, including the scrutiny companies get, the *liquidity* of their stock, whether they issue dividends, and the likelihood that they will grow.

Liquidity matters, since it determines how easy or tough it might be to find a buyer for an investment you want to sell.

**liquidity**
a measure of whether a ready and willing market for the investment you want to buy or sell exists.

## Big Blues

Blue-chip stocks are issued by companies worth $5 billion or more. The term "blue chip" was taken from poker, where the blue chips are the most valuable.

Blue-chip companies typically receive extensive attention from the media and are followed by Wall Street and brokerage firm analysts. The stocks are easy to buy and sell and their prices are often a little high because there is little risk that these corporations will fail. You can expect dividends from many blue chips, but not always meaningful growth potential. This is where your investment strategy comes into play. You should ask and answer the question: Why am I investing? If you're already in retirement or need to use your investments for current income, blue-chip companies that are unlikely to grow very much but that do pay dividends may be a good choice for your money.

These stocks are liquid and are traded on the American Stock Exchange (AMEX), New York Stock Exchange (NYSE), and, to a lesser extent, the Nasdaq Stock Market. The *indexes* that track or benchmark the average performance of this group as a whole include the Dow Jones Industrial Average, the S&P 500, and the Wilshire 5000 (for more on these indexes and benchmarks, see Chapter 7).

**index**
an average; a gauge of a particular market based on the computation of the average prices or price movement of a group of like investments.

## Middle of the Road

Mid-cap stocks are issued by companies with a *capitalization* of $1 billion to $5 billion. They get some scrutiny from the media and brokerage firm analysts and are fairly liquid and easy to trade. The potential for growth is better than it is for most blue-chip stocks precisely because there is a bit more risk. You're also less likely to be paid dividends, which is a consideration if you're looking for immediate income. These stocks are traded on the American, New York, and Nasdaq stock exchanges. One of the indexes that track or benchmark the average performance of this group as a whole is the Russell Mid-Cap Index.

**capitalization**
the total value of issues of a company's stock; equals the number of shares outstanding multiplied by the price.

## Opportunities on the Small Side

Small-cap stocks are issued by companies with a capitalization of $1 billion or less and receive little if any media or brokerage analyst coverage until the price has risen dramatically—or, as some more jaded investors might put it, when the horse is already out of the barn. That phrase insinuates that the stock has nowhere to go but down; however, stocks such as Amazon.com have proven that isn't always an accurate analysis or depiction of small caps in the process of metamorphosing into large caps.

There is potentially less liquidity and ease of trading, especially for obscure or little-known stocks, than for well-known stocks. While big gains are possible from small-cap stocks, you take on higher risk that a company will stumble and even fail than you do with mid-cap or blue-chip stocks. That's because they often have more debt and less operating capital. As a result, they have less room for error and less of an ability to ride out downturns in the economy, their industry, or their market. At the same time, small companies can be lithe and quick on their feet, sometimes finding and exploiting product and service niches much more quickly and profitably than larger companies tend to.

Small-cap stocks are traded on Nasdaq or the *over-the-counter market*. That latter got its name when stock was literally bought over the counter at brokerage firms, like a nonprescription medicine is bought over the counter at a drugstore. Today most stock orders are taken over the phone. Over-the-counter stocks are not required to meet the same requirements for capitalization, earnings, or size that listed stocks must meet. The index that tracks or benchmarks the average performance of this group as a whole is the Russell 2000 Index.

## Ups and Downs

Stocks don't provide investors with any guarantees, and values can change dramatically over time; but stocks have historically proven to be the single most profitable investment going, beating bonds, cash, precious metals, real estate, and all other legitimate investments. Ibbotson Associates, Inc., a Chicago-based market tracking firm, found that stocks have beaten inflation by seven percentage points since World War II. Compare that to bonds, which have beaten inflation by just two percentage points, and Treasury bills, which outpaced inflation by just one percentage point. Since World War II, there have been only two five-calendar-year periods (1970–1974 and 1973–1977) when owning stocks would have cost you money.

And here's another note to those who think it wise to flee a sinking ship: One of the best ways historically to minimize losses has not been to sell stock when its price has decreased. The smartest move historically for investors hit with a down market has been to ride out the storm and stay invested, since the prices of most stocks eventually rose and made investors whole.

Prices rise and fall based on supply and demand. You can find the prices of publicly traded stocks every day in most daily newspapers and on many online web sites, such as Yahoo! and America Online.

> **over-the-counter market** a market for exchanging stocks in which the shares are bought over the counter at brokerage firms, as opposed to being listed on a stock exchange.

### Why Common Beats Preferred

Investors can buy either common or preferred stock. Common stock can rise or fall in value and pay a varying dividend or no dividend at all, depending on the market for that particular stock. Preferred stock pays a guaranteed dividend, so there is reduced risk, but also reduced reward. Unlike a common stock shareholder, you won't receive a larger dividend payment if company profits increase. In addition, your shares will appreciate more slowly. Owning preferred stock, though, does put you ahead of common shareholders when it comes to receiving dividend payments or in the unlikely event the company goes bankrupt and you find yourself in line for a share of the liquidated assets. In most instances, however, you don't have voting rights as do common stock owners.

## THE BUZZ ABOUT BONDS

A bond is a document that represents debt that a company or government issues. Companies routinely offer bonds for sale as a means of raising money to pay for expansion or modernization, to cover expenses, or to finance corporate takeovers. Government entities—both the federal government and states, counties, and towns—issue bonds to pay for government activities; to finance public projects such as building schools, highways, or stadia; or to pay off debt. While corporations can issue either stocks or bonds to raise money, they sometimes prefer to issue bonds so they won't dilute, or lessen, the value of stock already owned by investors.

**coupon rate**
the amount of interest that is paid to bondholders. The coupon rate can be fixed or floating.

Investors often buy bonds for the income they produce. You buy a bond, hold it to maturity, and receive fixed interest payments at regular intervals—usually once or twice a year. That's why bonds are called fixed-income securities. Then, when the bond matures, you get your principal back. If you buy a bond at less than par (its face value), and sell it for more than par, you can earn a substantial profit.

There are also risks. If interest rates go up, buyers may end up receiving less money because the bonds they are holding don't pay as much as newer bonds that are being issued. The alternative, to sell before the bond matures, may be equally risky since the seller may not get back what he or she paid for the bond. Inflation can also take its toll on long-term bonds, because the value of what the bonds pay will be eroded over time.

When you buy a bond you get a document or coupon that shows the amount of the bond, the interest rate that will be paid, the term of repayment of the principle, and par value (what you receive when the bond matures). The *coupon rate* is the amount of interest a bondholder receives; it is expressed as a percentage of par value. The maturity date is when the bondholder gets his or her principal back.

Bonds are sold by brokers and sometimes banks and come in four types: Treasuries, corporate bonds, tax-exempt municipal bonds, and *mortgage-backed bonds*.

Bonds are called fixed-income securities because their interest income is set, or fixed, when the bond is sold. Bonds that are held to full term are said to "mature." Those which the borrower (issuer) prepays are said to have been "called." There is risk in owning bonds, since the borrower may not pay back the loan (your principal). And because bonds are bought and sold, they can rise and fall in value as market conditions change. But bonds issued by the U.S. government, by most state and local governments, and by topflight corporations are usually safe from default, so you can expect to get your principal back, though you may not receive any interest or profit.

As an indication of how risky bonds are, they are rated by national rating services such as Moody's and Standard & Poor's. Generally, the higher the *rating* a bond gets, the lower the interest rate it will pay investors.

As a rule, bonds are used to diversify an investor's portfolio and reduce risk, because they act contrary to the stock market. In effect, bonds often hold steady or increase in value when the stock market is falling or interest rates are rising. Bonds can also offer tax advantages, since states and other municipalities can issue tax-free bonds that pay interest that investors don't have to count for income tax purposes. While that sounds like free money, bear in mind that sometimes tax-advantaged bonds pay

**mortgage-backed bonds**
bonds issued by three government-sponsored entities, the Government National Mortgage Association, the Federal National Mortgage Association, and the Federal Home Loan Mortgage Corporation (Ginnie Maes, Fannie Maes, and Freddie Macs, respectively). They are backed by pools of mortgages that the associations buy, package, and sell on the secondary market.

**rating**
a measure of how safe from default a bond is. Generally, a rating of A or above from such services as Moody's, Standard & Poor's, and Fitch's Investment Service is considered acceptable.

less than taxable bonds may end up paying you on an af-
ter-tax basis, so make sure you do the math or check with
your accountant to see which investment will actually add
more to your bottom line.

Bonds can provide higher returns than certificates
of deposit (CDs) and other cash equivalents, but bonds
are not backed by *federal deposit insurance*. So if the en-
tity issuing the bond goes belly-up, you could lose your
money.

## CASH EQUIVALENTS: A DIFFERENT KIND OF MONEY MARKET

Money market mutual funds offer a safe haven for
money that investors need to use in the next five years.
But they are not like money market funds offered by a
bank, which federally insure investors against loss in exchange for paying a lower interest rate. The principal
you invest in a money market mutual fund is not guaranteed or insured against loss, but these funds pay
higher rates than banks do. It's also worth noting that no
money market mutual fund has ever defaulted on investors. Every dollar you put in you can expect to get
back, plus interest. Shop around for the most competitive rates, which become higher or lower in tandem with
interest rates in general. As an added convenience, most
fund companies allow investors to write checks on their
money market mutual fund accounts, which makes
these very liquid accounts.

### Other Cash Equivalents

A cash equivalent is an asset or investment that can be so
quickly converted to dollars that it is essentially the
equivalent of cash. A money market mutual fund is a cash
equivalent that is not federally insured. A certificate of deposit (CD) is an example of a cash equivalent that *is* federally insured. You can purchase a CD through your bank.
In exchange for the federal insurance, you get paid only a
small amount of interest and you have to agree to lock in

**federal deposit insurance**
insurance a bank
issuing debt buys
from the federal
government to
protect investors
against loss.
Federally insured
investments are
safer than others,
but generally pay
a lower rate.
Bonds are not
backed by this
insurance.

your money for a specific period, usually six months to 10 years. The longer you agree to lock in your money, the higher the rate you'll be paid. Be certain that you won't need your money early, since all banks charge an early withdrawal penalty if you cash out before the term of the CD has expired.

## YOUR INVESTMENT OF CHOICE

If you come from a family that has made investing a family affair and you already have some experience analyzing and selecting individual stocks or bonds to invest in, or you are willing to do the homework it takes, stocks or bonds may be a comfortable choice for you as you start your investment plan.

If, however, you don't want to analyze or track the performance of individual companies, and instead prefer the thought of choosing a mutual fund money manager who has a decent track record of doing that for investors, mutual funds will probably work better for you. Either way, the important thing here is that you're on the road to getting started.

## YOUR TRADING OPTIONS

The least expensive way to buy mutual fund shares is from the mutual fund company itself, directly. Almost all have toll-free phone numbers you can get by calling the toll-free directory (800-555-1212) or searching for the fund family online. If you buy fund shares, stocks, or bonds from a broker, financial planner, or insurance agent, you will pay a commission or a fee (or sometimes both) for the service. Commissions on stocks and bonds are usually set at a specific dollar amount depending on the number of shares you're purchasing. However, commissions you can be charged on mutual funds can range as high as 5.75%; this can really eat up your principal and shave future performance. So, whenever possible, buy direct from the fund company.

| TABLE 3.2 What You'll Pay to Trade through a Broker | | | | |
|---|---|---|---|---|
| Broker | 200 Shares | 500 Shares | 1,000 Shares | Annual Fee |
| Merrill Lynch | $129 | $225 | $308 | $35 |
| Schwab | $89 | $106.60 | $123.60 | $29 |
| Fidelity | $113 | $155 | $165 | $24 |
| Waterhouse | $35 | $57.62 | $90.33 | $0 |

Most investors purchase investments through a brokerage firm, either in person, over the phone, or online. There are a variety of different types of brokerage firms—from deep-discount brokers that may charge you as little as $14 to buy or sell your order for stock shares to full-service firms that might recommend stocks and provide corresponding research on the companies. In between are the brokerage supermarkets such as Charles Schwab and Waterhouse Securities, which offer a minimum of assistance and some online research, albeit at a reduced price. Most firms also charge an annual fee. Both commissions and fees can really vary, so do a bit of comparison shopping and understand that if you trade often, the commissions you pay will eat up your profits. (See Table 3.2.)

Investors also have the option of purchasing stocks directly from a growing number of companies that have set up direct reinvestment programs (called DRIPs). To find out if a company offers a DRIP, call its investor relations department. As a pragmatic matter, most shares are held by the brokerage firm; it is rare today for individuals to hold individual stock certificates themselves.

# The 10 Things You Must Know about Your Investments

You could try to know everything about every sector of the investment world. It makes sense if you believe knowledge equals power. But you'll quickly discover there are reams and reams, to use an increasingly old-fashioned term, of facts out there. You're also likely to find a bevy of investors, journalists, and market gurus touting the next must-have investment every time you turn around. There are so many facts and factoids and opinions out there that you'll probably feel like you have to put waders on just to get through them all.

1. Mutual funds.
2. Stocks.
3. Bonds.
4. Tracking.
5. Good and bad news.
6. Daily habits.
7. Volatility.
8. Earnings estimates.
9. Changing of the guard.
10. Hot products.

You've got a life presumably filled with plenty of other activities. You want to devote time to your investments, but you can't afford to have your every waking moment consumed, either. You need a way to make your search more efficient, a method for editing out all that stuff you don't need so you can concentrate on what is essential. We'll start this process with a look at what you absolutely, positively need to know to create and manage a portfolio of investments.

## GETTING DOWN TO BASICS

There is a base, a core of knowledge, that is critical to your success. Once we've outlined what constitutes the base of knowledge you'll need, we'll move on to some definitions. (If we say you need to know about total return, it won't make sense unless you know what we're talking about.) Then we'll launch our search across the great divide of information sources available to investors.

There are a dozen places you could start your research. You can begin with the big picture, looking at the economy and deciding which parts of it are doing well, then pinpoint stocks in those sectors that look like they are benefitting or may benefit soon from the boom. Or you can feed a set of factors into an online or CD-ROM database and see what investments the program spits out—for instance, "The Top 10 Best Performing Blue Chip Stocks" or "The 10 Hottest Aggressive Growth Mutual Funds." Using these programs you can slice and dice performance data any way you want. For instance, you might ask the program to show you only companies with 20% annual earnings growth and a share price under $50. Or you can "buy the charts," which means using the movement of share prices, usually up, as your signal to invest.

In a classic buy-what-you-know strategy, you can act on your inclinations—say, your liking for burgers prompts you to check out McDonald's. Fidelity's famous fund manager (and now ad spokesman) Peter Lynch made thousands of Magellan Fund investors wealthy using this strategy.

Another investing strategy is as close as home. You can be true to your home state and buy its bonds, or mutual funds that invest in its bonds, because you believe your state is economically sound and will be a good credit risk. Besides, if you're a resident you'll get a tax break. You can also buy the stocks of companies that are in your own backyard or even buy shares of a mutual fund that specializes in the companies operating in a single state or a region.

You can decide that any mutual fund with low fees and expenses that mirrors an index of the stock market is the key to investing. When stocks are moving up, this investment strategy can produce shining results, as it did during most of the 1990s. But you have to understand the downside as well: When indexes do poorly, so do index mutual funds that invest in the underlying investments.

You might also want to look at demographic trends— what the population at large is doing. There are few populations in the United States larger than baby boomers, who number a mind-boggling 76 million. What they do or don't do has a profound impact on the U.S. economy and the investment markets, says Harvard-trained economist and money manager William Sterling, who argues that "boomers' demand for stocks could support high stock prices for years to come."

## MUST-KNOW INFO

Each of these methods is accepted by huge numbers of investors. But as simple as they all sound, smart investors should go beyond an overly simplistic investment style and use basic research and analysis to refine their investment selections and ultimately make the right investment choice. Choosing a mutual fund just because it invests in an index won't do you much good if the fund has higher expenses and a worse performance than any of its competitors.

The same is true of stocks and bonds. Just because you choose an investment in your backyard doesn't mean, for instance, that it isn't significantly riskier or being outperformed by other investments. Gathering relevant information will allow you to fully analyze an investment and steer clear of knee-jerk decisions. Depending on which investment you select, the most basic of research you need to pull together includes the following information:

### A Mutual Fund Picker's Primer

• *Investment objective.* Mutual funds have to disclose their objective, which will give an indication of how much risk you can expect. It is important for you to know what the fund's strategy is because you're trying to build a diversified portfolio.

• *One-, three-, and five-year performance.* When you consider a mutual fund, you're looking at the underlying performance of the holdings in its portfolio, be they stocks, bonds, real estate investment trusts, or cash. To assess how the fund fared compared to its competitors, compare one-, three-, and five-year performance to a suitable benchmark, such as the S&P 500 Index or the Merrill Lynch bond index, or to a peer group of other similar stocks or mutual funds. Checking three periods keeps you from buying flash-in-the-pan performers.

• *Track record in volatile markets.* How does the fund do in down markets? In up markets? Does it give up a bit of performance in order to minimize risk? Volatility is what keeps you up nights wondering if you were nuts to have put good money into a fund. Knowing beforehand what you could be in for helps you sleep better, so take a look at the fund's historical track record, say over the past five years. If it doesn't have one, check on similar funds and see how they performed in volatile markets.

• *Manager.* Who is the manager and how long has she or he been in charge? You are buying a track record. Be sure the manager who is in charge now is responsible for that record. Otherwise, you're buying memories, not dreams or potential.

• *Expenses.* How much are expenses? In a down market, expenses can become a hindrance to performance. The bull market of the late 1990s swept aside the very important issue of expenses. Short-term, and in hot markets, you'll hear some investors say, "Who cares, as long as performance is good?" when asked what it's costing them to invest in a particular fund. But over the long term, expenses really eat into gains. "There is growing research that shows that low-expense funds tend to do better than high-expense funds over time," says John Rekanthaler, research director at Morningstar Mutual Funds, Chicago.

Articles on fund costs on www.Morningstar.com, as well as www.Vanguard.com's web site section entitled "Comparing Mutual Fund Costs," are both not-to-be-missed sources of information that demonstrate beyond a shadow of doubt how much fund costs impact performance over time.

• *Minimum investment.* Minimums range from $50 or even less for retirement accounts to $1 million, depending on the market a fund group caters to. If the minimum a fund requires is too high, move it to a back burner until you accumulate more assets. Bear in mind, however, that you may be able to lower the minimum investment by using a discount broker such as Charles Schwab or Waterhouse Securities. In addition, if you want the fund for an IRA, you may be in luck. Many funds lower the minimum for IRA retirement accounts, typically to $2,000. Other funds often allow you to start investing, even in nonretirement accounts, if you set up an automatic investment plan that directs your bank to send the fund company a set amount each month.

## A Stock Picker's Primer

• *Company profiles.* No matter how technical an investor you are and how much you buy the charts, you still need to know the nuts and bolts of the companies you invest in. You want to know what a company does and where it operates.

## A World of Mutual Funds to Choose From

Mutual funds come in all stripes and sizes depending on investment objective. You shouldn't invest in one just because it is doing well. You must know how it got that gain so you can determine if it fits into your investment strategy.

One caution: Don't judge a fund by its name alone. Fund managers are sometimes given wide latitude as to what they can invest in. As a result, a value fund will often contain plenty of growth-oriented investments. A small-cap fund might include some mighty large companies. And global funds may invest in a very high percentage of U.S. stocks when that market is booming.

It's best when you do your research to look beyond the fund name to the style analysis provided by Morningtar and Value Line, as well as how magazines and newspapers categorize the funds. These will be more accurate, if broad-brush, indicators of what the fund owns. Then, as we'll discuss in Chapter 6, you'll need to get down to it and check a fund's actual portfolio holdings to make your decision.

Here are the major fund types. If you're interested in buying mutual funds, you'll choose from these to build a portfolio that reflects your risk tolerance and a diversified asset mix.

**Aggressive Growth Funds.** *Aggressive growth funds* go searching for the stocks of new companies, small companies, and undervalued companies they expect to increase in value. What that translates to is that you're running the risk of above-average losses in return for the possibility of above-average gains. These funds can also be called capital appreciation funds.

**Growth Funds.** *Growth funds* are the engines of long-term gain. These funds own mostly big or

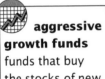

**aggressive growth funds**
funds that buy the stocks of new companies, small companies, and undervalued companies they expect to increase in value.

**growth funds**
funds that own mostly big or medium-sized companies that look for long-term gain.

medium-sized companies that were on a roll, with rising earnings, through most of the 1990s. If you're looking for dividends, forget it. Growth stocks are in it for capital gains; that is, they want their share price to rise, often dramatically, on the prospect of continuing growth. The risk is bear markets, which can pound these funds hard.

**Medium Company Growth Funds.** *Medium company growth funds*, also called mid-cap funds, specialize in finding medium-sized companies, most often defined as those whose market capitalization—the number of shares outstanding times the share price—is under $5 billion. The promise in this arena, at least for the short term, is that mid-cap companies are less followed than large- and small-cap companies, so there may be more of a chance of finding an unknown winner. Also, they provide an additional diversification tool, since they act differently from both large- and small-cap companies when there is a down market. If you're buying a mid-cap fund to diversify your portfolio, make sure that it actually has mid-cap funds in its own portfolio. You don't want a fund that has mostly large-cap holdings.

**medium company growth funds** funds that specialize in medium-sized companies whose market capitalization is under $5 billion. Also called mid-cap funds.

**Small Company Growth Funds.** *Small company growth funds*, also called small-cap funds, build portfolios from the stock of small companies, most often defined as those whose market capitalization—the number of shares outstanding times the share price—is under $1 billion. Small-cap stocks and funds are cyclical, though over time they have outperformed large-cap stocks. For instance, they boomed in the early 1990s, then lagged the market in the latter half of the decade. Investors hold small-cap funds as a way to diversify. But you'll need to hold on to these investments for longer periods, at least five years and more, to catch the rising, profitable cycles.

**small company growth funds** funds that specialize in small companies whose market capitalization is under $1 billion. Also called small-cap funds.

*(Continued)*

**value funds**
funds that look for bargain, or underpriced, stocks that fund managers believe will rise in the future.

 **equity income funds**
funds that seek dividend income and slightly more growth than growth and income funds. Their underlying investments are blue-chip stocks, with some utilities for dividends.

 **balanced funds**
funds whose portfolios are made up of about 60% stocks and 40% bonds.

**Value Funds.** *Value funds* have portfolios filled with bargains, also called underpriced stocks, which the fund managers believe will rise again. You have to hang on to value funds. They aren't highfliers when the market is booming, but in a down market they can move up and are much more likely to hold their value. Even in a very bad bear market, you're likely to lose less with value funds than you are with riskier funds. That's why they're a good diversification tool. Over time, they can outperform growth stocks. And they carry higher dividend yields than growth stocks.

**Growth and Income Funds.** These funds are the home of the blue chips. Their portfolios are meant to provide steady growth and pay high dividends. Since they usually carry only an average risk of loss, you can also use them to diversify a more aggressive growth portfolio.

**Equity Income Funds.** *Equity income funds* are designed to deliver dividend income and a tad more growth than growth and income funds. Their underlying investments are blue-chip stocks, with some utilities thrown in for purposes of paying dividends. The risk with equity income funds is about average.

**Balanced Funds.** *Balanced funds* have both stocks and bonds in their portfolios, which are usually made up of about 60% stocks and 40% bonds. Investors own these funds to help them through bear markets during which they deliver dividend and interest income.

**Income Funds.** Providing income, but very little growth, *income funds* invest primarily in bonds, but may buy some dividend-paying stocks. There is limited risk of loss, but your money may have a hard time beating or even keeping up with inflation, which costs investors about 3% a year in spending power every year in the 1990s.

**Bond Funds.** *Bond funds* invest in all different types of bonds, depending on what a fund's investment objective is. There are steady income funds that invest in U.S. Treasury bonds and those issued by government agencies. Some funds specialize in municipal bonds, and others in a variety of bonds that have maturities of between one and 10 years. Some even invest in junk bonds, so you'd take on much higher risk than you would with the usual bond fund.

**Sector Funds.** These funds specialize in a sector of the economy. Two of the better-known types of sector funds invest in companies that specialize in technology or provide financial services. The stocks of banks, insurance companies, and brokerage firms would make up the portfolio of the latter. Through much of the bull market of the 1990s, sector funds showed big gains. But you have to expect ups and downs since these sectors—and, alas, these funds—are highly volatile. Tech funds can soar 50% or more in a fiscal year, and just as easily crash, as they did in late 1998 when the market turned with a vengeance on technology stocks.

**International, World, and Global Funds.** These funds invest in a portfolio of non-U.S. stocks and/or bonds. They may also, as is the case with world and global funds, invest in the U.S. markets as well. The funds with international holdings can provide decent diversity for those who hold U.S. stocks and bonds, since there is evidence that foreign and U.S. markets do not move in lockstep with each other. The risk of these holdings is market risk, in addition to currency fluctuation.

*(Continued)*

 **income funds**
funds that invest primarily in bonds and dividend-paying stocks.

 **bond funds**
funds that invest only in bonds, and may specialize in certain types of bonds based on the investment objective.

**index funds**
funds that invest in the stocks that make up a particular index. Their performance mirrors that of the overall market.

**Index Funds.** For many mutual fund investors, keeping it simple is a major goal. That's part of the attraction of *index funds*. These stock mutual funds' holdings are meant to mirror a financial index, such as the S&P 500, so they invest in the stocks that make up the index. There are more than 150 different mutual funds that track almost every known index for small, mid-cap, and large companies, as well as bond market and international indexes. Because they track the stock market overall, instead of the performance of individual companies as a regular mutual fund would, these funds are easier for investors to monitor. When the stock market dips, however, as it did in 1987 to the tune of more than 20%, stock index funds can be hit hard.

As you begin your research, you'll be amazed at the number of U.S. companies that have operations abroad or make unrelated products and services you had no idea they produced. As a result, you'll also want to know if a company has any subsidiaries or partnerships that may have a bearing on the future value of its stock. Just because a company produces orange juice profitably in the United States doesn't mean that the semiconductor business it just acquired in Brussels will fare as well.

**investor relations department**
a department in a company you can call to obtain annual reports, quarterly reports, and company updates.

You need names, an address, and telephone numbers at the company, usually in the *investor relations department*, in order to get copies of annual reports, quarterly reports, and company updates. Having a phone number in the investor relations department will also give you a place to call if you have a question about news regarding the company, its products, or share performance.

• *Historical performance.* Speaking of performance, measuring it for a given investment is a key initial step of your research. It's important that you look at performance over a period of time to see how the price of a stock has fluctuated. Since buying low is your goal, you'll want to know the highs and lows so you can set target prices for buying and, if you desire, selling shares. Buying low means you believe the price of the stock will go up. The fact that it has already doubled or tripled its price recently is not a reason to buy, unless you believe the price can go higher. If you know the highs and lows of the stock price you'll also be better prepared for any fluctuation you're likely to experience if you invest in the stock. This fluctuation is also referred to as volatility.

Take a look at a company's revenues, profit margins, and earnings growth over time as well, because they are the nuts and bolts of evaluating a company, even one whose burgers you love.

• *Timely price quotes.* If you set target prices at which you will buy or sell, you need to follow the prices of stocks so you'll be able to take advantage of the peaks and valleys of the markets. You also have to track the performance of your holdings to know whether your investments are meeting your goals.

## A Bond Picker's Primer

• *Bond rating.* Dun & Bradstreet, Moody's, and Standard & Poor's investigate the financial condition of bond issuers and then give them ratings of AAA down to D. The AAA ratings are usually awarded to blue-chip companies and well-run municipalities. Bonds with these ratings are investment grade, so you have fairly solid assurances that you'll get your money back. Don't think of buying anything with a rating below BBB or Baa. Bonds with these ratings have some speculative elements to them, and while they're able to pay interest to their current bondholders, they may be at risk of default. Any bonds rated CCC or below are junk bonds, named so by investors. These lowest-rated bonds are highly speculative and have poor prospects of repaying investors—though if you're willing to take the risk, these bonds can pay yields almost as good as what you get on a good, safe blue-chip stock.

Remember, too, that rating firms such as Standard & Poor's are rating an issuer based on its financial condition. They look at an issuer's overall debt, how fast the issuer's revenues and profits are growing, how it compares to competitors, and the state of the economy. Their job is to alert investors to the potential of an issuer defaulting. While that's vitally important, the rating says nothing about whether investors are buying the bonds. So don't mistake a rating for any type of guarantee.

Rating firms assign ratings to corporate, municipal and international bonds; U.S. Treasury bonds are not rated because they're obligations of the federal government and assumed to be solid as a rock. Only the highest-rated issuers make their ratings public. If you can't get the rating from the issuer, get it from a broker or the rating agency.

• *Par value.* This is the dollar amount of the bond at the time it was issued. Par value represents the amount originally paid for the bond and the amount that will be repaid when the bond matures. Most bonds are sold in multiples of $1,000. A bond can be bought and sold a number of times during its lifetime for an amount less or greater than its par value, depending on demand and market conditions.

• *Yield.* The interest rate, also known as the coupon rate, paid on the bonds is calculated as a percentage of the par value and is paid as interest (for Treasury bonds) or when the bond comes due (corporate bonds). If you hold the bond to maturity, you'll receive a yield similar to the interest rate. If the bond is traded before maturity, the yield could change. If the buyer paid more than par, the yield will be reduced. If he or she paid less, the yield will be increased. This is the reason you invest, so you have to know what the reward is for loaning an issuer your money.

• *Maturity date.* When will the bond be paid off? This is the year the bond comes due and must be repaid. Bonds are issued for a set period though they can be called, or bought back, by the issuer early.

## THINK LIKE AN INVESTOR

To get you thinking like an investor, there is information beyond some of these core measurements that you can use to monitor stocks in your portfolio and those on your *watch list.*

Perhaps you're waiting for the price to fall on a mutual fund or stock, or want to see how an investment reacts to industry and economic news or how it performs over time. To do that, you watch for price and performance information or company news that gives you the kind of insight you're looking for. You can also track stocks and mutual funds every weekday in the stock pages of your daily newspaper or go online to tracking services such as www.morningstar.net; America Online.com's personal finance section; TheStreet.com; or even the *Wall Street Journal's* online news site (www.wsj.com), which contains a daily archive of investment prices and performance.

 **watch list**
a list of investments that you find interesting enough to monitor their day-to-day performance.

## THE GOOD, BAD, AND UGLY

Both good and bad news can give you insight into how a company is faring. As for good news: You might see a TV show that talks about how the pharmaceutical company you're watching seems to be winning the competitive battle to be the first to introduce the latest painkiller. Not-so-good-news can include lawsuits against a company on your watch list, as well as scrutiny from regulators, such as the Securities and Exchange Commission, the Justice Department, or even the Food and Drug Administration. News can come in a variety of forms that can help you make decisions to buy, sell, or hold on to those assets you have. Sometimes people sell when the fundamentals on the basis of which they bought have changed. Other investors may see bad news as a short-term setback and an opportunity to pick up stock or mutual fund shares at a lower price.

## HONE YOUR HABITS

As you begin to consider different types of investments, your daily habits can be a significant tool in your quest for sound information and analysis. Whether it's the newspapers and magazines you read, the nightly news you watch, or any online research you do, your quest for knowledge can provide you with valuable information about what's going on inside a company, an industry, or an economy. Here is a taste of the type of news that should start catching your ear and eye—breaking developments like hiring, firings, and lawsuits.

Legendary turnaround specialist Al Dunlap's removal from national bread maker Sunbeam Corporation following questions about its revenues and profits pummeled share prices in 1998. Of course, the fact that his appointment two years earlier more than tripled share prices (up over 166%) had made Sunbeam many investors' darling. Not surprisingly, Dunlap's reputation was tarnished following the Sunbeam debacle. It's important to remember, however, that when heavy hitters take over a company or, conversely, are sacked by a company, it can trigger significant fluctuation in a stock's share price.

Cendant Corporation, whose businesses include Ramada, Howard Johnson, Avis, and Coldwell Banker, also suffered a major setback in 1998 when its books turned to mush and a spate of shareholder lawsuits followed. Share prices tumbled almost immediately. Keeping on top of breaking developments can save your portfolio from falling along with some executive's fortunes or tumbling into the abyss that questionable bookkeeping and accounting can create.

On the good-news front, there was the return of Steve Jobs to computer maker Apple in 1997, a move that alone boosted share prices for months before the successful introduction of new computers like the iMac in 1998, which took the stock price from less than $20 to more than $40.

## UP, DOWN, AND BACK UP AGAIN

Of course, you don't have to sell if you believe the news you're hearing will have only a short-term negative bearing on a company's stock price. You may even want to buy.

Microsoft's seemingly endless battles with the Justice Department over antitrust issues managed to nick shares from time to time, but overall, Microsoft stock continued to climb in value into 1999. It slid below $45, but bounced back up to over $80 in early 1999. It's hard to sell a stock that has made so many people rich. At the same time, Microsoft shareholders know the implications of a probe of this magnitude could threaten the value of their holdings, especially if the company is forced to divest itself of certain core businesses or profit-center technologies.

## THOSE DARN EARNINGS ESTIMATES

The market doesn't always act logically and punish companies that fall short of *earnings expectations* while rewarding those that exceed them. But forecasts of surprises concerning a company's earnings can impact stock prices. Usually, Wall Street is pretty unforgiving when a company announces it will not measure up to estimates. It can, however, reward companies that surprise us with higher than expected earnings results. If you've got your finger on the buy/sell trigger of a given stock, this year's earnings estimates and how close a company appears to be to hitting them should be a significant consideration.

Here is an example of how Wall Street's reaction will not always make sense. Yahoo! reported better than expected earnings late in 1998 and still got hammered

**earnings expectations**
an estimate of a company's earnings. Falling short of these estimates or exceeding them can greatly influence the price of the company's stock.

as larger concerns over the fate of technical stocks overshadowed its good news. Then the price of the stock turned around—from less than $40 a share to up over $200 in early 1999.

## WHO'S COMING ABOARD?

Beyond high-profile ups and downs of rainmakers like Jobs and Dunlap, the mere changing of the guard can be important for companies, even when it's planned and long anticipated. Watch the orderly transition—most times— at the big automakers for an example of smooth succession. What's important, though, is to know the style of the new leadership. For instance, Chrysler CEO Robert Lutz had car grease in his veins. At the opposite end of the spectrum, General Motors CEO John Smith was a number cruncher. Analysts who follow the auto industry peg Smith's penchant for accounting over product as one of the leading causes of General Motors' disappointing performance in the late 1990s.

For an example of how the question of succession can hang over a company, take a look at Disney. Michael Eisner's repeated failure to find a number two he can live with has become part of Wall Street's analysis of the company. And with Eisner's bypass surgery several years ago reminding investors of his mortality, it is not an idle concern. Without his leadership the company would be left rudderless, which is not exactly the best thing to be in the cutthroat entertainment industry.

## HOT PRODUCTS

You can find information on new products and services in almost every reference mentioned in this book. When things are sailing along smoothly, sometimes it's difficult to see the connection between the launch of a new product and a company stock. But new products can save companies. Innovative services can revive them. (Conversely, clunkers can hurt strong companies and take down weak ones.)

Volkswagen shed its long-running stock price doldrums with one new product: the new, improved Beetle.

NBC's long-running success, the drama series *ER*, is believed by both analysts and NBC executives to be a major component of the success of the network's stock. To preserve the show and keep its stars happy, the network gave each of them a $1 million present in 1998—much as a profitable company might reward its executives for a good year.

Drugmaker Pfizer's stock soared as a result of the success of its anti-impotence drug Viagra, up from $34 to more than $130.

As we've said, information on products can be found every day in newspapers and magazines. But it is also available, and useful, when you get it from the source, the company itself. The web sites maintained by companies such as Compaq (www.compaq.com), Dell Computer (www.dell.com), and IBM (www.ibm.com) all offer comprehensive descriptions of their product offerings, as well as press releases about new products, personnel, restructuring, and financial news. The more you know about them, the savvier you'll be as an investor. Because you'll not only know where stocks on your watch list stand in relation to your expectations, but you'll also know where they stand in relation to their competitors. A new product isn't much to write home about if it can't match the bells and whistles of a competitor's new offering that has already captured 90% of existing market share.

## CAREER AND BUSINESS OPPORTUNITIES

You wouldn't be the first investor whose confidence in a company extended beyond owning stock. Often in the course of learning about a company you may discover a career opportunity. Many companies and other organizations post job openings on their web sites. That's the case with America Online (www.aol.com), Fannie Mae (www.fanniemae.com), and the Securities and Exchange Commission (www.sec.org), which all offer extensive listings of the jobs they have open.

You might also find business opportunities. Companies like AT&T, Microsoft, and IBM have alliances with many small businesses to whom they subcontract work. If you're a small business owner, knowing of such opportunities and possible alliances could make a huge difference in the success of your company.

*Chapter*

# 5

# How Analysts
# Look at Investments

■■■■■■■■■

A s shocking as it seems, facts aren't overflowing with value in and of themselves. Facts need to be put into context to have meaning to investors. Put another way, we don't know how blue a sky really is unless we've seen other blue skies, and maybe even gray skies, too. As new investors, we don't know how profitable a company is, either, or whether its stock price is a bargain, or whether it can continue to compete successfully in its market unless we have a way of comparing and contrasting pertinent facts within the context of the company's industry, economy, and competitive situation.

At the same time you can't just follow the crowd and hope you'll score big without doing your homework. "It's just not good enough to buy what everyone else is buying anymore, especially with more volatile asset classes [like high technology and international stocks]," says Catherine Somhegyi, chief investment officer at Nicholas-Applegate Capital Management, San Diego.

## HOW ANALYSIS WORKS

Professional investors and paid analysts—the latter can earn tons of money crunching this kind of information for brokerage firms, mutual fund companies, or any other financial institutions that have to make investment choices—adopt styles of analysis to give context and meaning to the information they gather and process. You've no doubt read what some have to say in newspapers and magazines and you've probably seen some on TV explaining good or bad turns in the market and maybe making predictions about what will happen in the coming days, months, or even years.

Simply put, formal analysis is a methodology for sorting information about the markets and individual investments, but not a surefire stock-picking tool. It's an analysts' filter, their way of looking at and assessing investment opportunities in relation to the other opportunities that are available, and to what's going on in the market, the economy, and with competitors. Knowing how different forms of analysis work will give you the ability to better decipher what analysts are saying and why. And it's a tool, really a set of tools, that you can use, too, to sharpen your investment selection.

Of course, there are no guarantees with investing. The value of stocks and their prices are not set by reality and what should be, but by investors' cumulative perception of reality and what they believe will be. So in essence, it is investors' interpretation of facts and what they believe they will mean to the future value of the company that determine how well or poorly a stock fares. There are no guarantees because no one we can find has created a crystal ball that will tell you what future events and changes companies will have to cope with or how investors will perceive the impact of these events and changes.

## EDUCATED CHOICES

Still, an educated guess, as you're learning, is far better when choosing an investment than making a wild stab in the dark. Analysis is one valid way that investors can improve their guesswork, by making sure they have the facts they believe are relevant to their decision. While analysis should be only one of several ways you double-check investments that interest you, it's a sound method for checking criteria you believe are important to selecting an investment that will be suitable to your goals, your risk tolerance, and your diversification plan.

## STYLES OF ANALYSIS

You've probably read or heard mutual fund managers expound on how they pick stocks, using words like value and growth, or bottom-up and top-down investing.

You've probably also heard spirited debates between analysts or investors who subscribe to a quantitative, or quant, style of investing, and those who are tire kickers. Don't get thrown by the jargon. The first style of investor relies on the numbers found in data about stocks; the second looks at products and management as the key to good investments. While these styles can seem contrary to one another—and purists would agree they are—there are plenty of investors who mix and mesh their analysis styles. The information that can be derived from different styles of analysis often actually complements each other, to provide a clearer view of your choices. There is only one, firm rule when it comes to analysis: You must select a style or develop one that works for you.

To understand the different styles available to you, and how they work, take a look at those that have evolved over the years.

### Fundamental Analysis

*Fundamental analysis* is both historical and predictive in nature. Analysts and investors who use fundamentals look at how fast a specific company's earnings are growing, along with sales, market share, dividends, and other financial measurements. Then, based on historical fundamentals, they attempt to make predictions about where a stock price is going.

This is as close as many investors come to Peter Lynch's buy-what-you-know approach, which includes not only financial analysis but a consideration of less

**fundamental analysis**
a method of stock analysis that focuses on past measures—such as a company's earnings, market share, or sales—to estimate what will happen to the price of that stock in the future.

tangible measures like how much stock in the company top management owns. Lynch, the former manager of Fidelity Investments' Magellan Fund, is still a consultant to the company and hawks their funds and services as lead spokesman (with Lily Tomlin and Don Rickles) in Fidelity's ads. When a manager owns stock in his or her own company it's a sign that people at the very center of the operation have confidence in the company where they work. Of course, when a company's top managers sell company stock, that sends an altogether different message.

A shake-up in the share price that Internet service provider America Online (AOL) endured in October 1998 was triggered when analysts and investors got wind that one senior manager was unloading one million shares. Share prices tumbled on that news alone.

Any report of financial results, predictions, and other facts or estimates related to value can be considered fundamental analysis. Factors such as a company's *balance sheet*, *income statement*, and *cash flow statement* report its status and the results of its operations, so these can be crucial measurements of a company's ability to do well in the future. Other factors? We'll look at these more closely in Chapter 6, but they include dividends paid, earnings per share, and *price-earnings ratios (P/Es)*, as well as trends in gross sales, gross profit margins, and net profits.

True fundamentalists also watch what's happening outside of a company's balance sheet, considering factors such as the quality of management, the quality of products and services, new product development, relative market share, cost-cutting initiatives, and mergers and acquisitions.

"We're focusing on stocks benefiting from corporate restructurings, privatization, globalization, and a focus on shareholder value," says Loretta Morris, a portfolio manager for Nicholas Applegate's International Core Growth mutual fund.

Fundamental analysis is best used as part of an overall method for selecting stocks, and ideally as a tool to identify and eliminate lesser alternatives, leaving a few good candidates standing to which you can apply other

**balance sheet**
statement of what a company owns (assets) and what it owes (liabilities) at the end of the year.

**income statement**
section of a financial statement that shows whether a company's operations turned a profit or generated a loss during the year.

**cash flow statement**
shows the company's cash balances after the cost of business activities are deducted.

standards including how well an overall industry is expected to do in the coming months and years.

Fundamental analysis tends to appeal to some high-profile fund managers like Robert Torray, manager of the Torray Fund, in Bethesda, Maryland, who rewarded investors with a five-year 24% return at the end of 1998. Torray tells his investors, analysts, and anyone else who will listen that what is important is "buying a company, not a stock." Torray is a star stock picker, and fundamental analysis works for star stock pickers in more ways than one. They want to know what's going on inside companies. And it allows such star stock pickers to hang their hats and their reputations on the handful of winning stocks they choose as a result of their analysis.

Technical stock pickers working with numbers and charts alone can't crow about the success of two or three star-maker stocks, since their focus is on their overall portfolio and number crunching, not the fundamentals of any one company.

It is in the fundamental camp that you find many growth and value investors, as well as income investors and those who seek to limit their stock picks to high-quality companies with long records of growth, otherwise known as blue-chip stocks.

**price-earnings ratio (P/E)** the price of a stock divided by the company's earnings per share for the past year. This ratio is considered by some to indicate whether a stock is overvalued or undervalued.

**Value versus Growth.** Perhaps the most well-known and widely acknowledged dividing line between fundamental analysts separates those who favor value investments and those who favor growth.

In broad terms, value investors look for bargains that are underpriced in relation to their competitors and, most importantly, in relation to their potential. Value investors don't swing for the fence like a home run hitter would. As a result, they were out of step with the market for the latter half of the 1990s, when much of the stock market was soaring despite being significantly overpriced from a value investor's viewpoint. At the same time, it was difficult to find stocks that were battered and underpriced—and still had a positive story to tell. Value investors, sometimes called bargain basement or flea market shoppers, may have had a difficult time finding great stocks in the late 1990s, but that doesn't mean that they haven't done well. Mutual Series Funds, a group of mutual funds managed by long-time value investor Michael Price and since 1998 by his successor, Robert Friedman, lagged the performance of growth funds for a few years in the late 1990s, but still managed to rack up excellent long-term performance that put it in the top 10 for growth and income mutual funds over both a 10- and a 15-year period. The point is that value and growth investing styles tend to go in and out of style over time.

In contrast, growth investors will pay above-average prices for a stock they think is growing at a better than average pace if they believe it's on track to keep growing. A number of stocks managed to do just that during the last decade of the twentieth century, against odds and many predictions. The question money managers kept asking was, "How much longer can this bull market continue? Can stocks go up forever?"

Unfortunately, a bull market *can't* go on forever. But that notion has been a difficult one for investors to grasp during the past decade when the bull has run forward, with nary a slowdown.

**Top-Down versus Bottom-Up.** These phrases refer to where analysts or investors begin their research to find good investments. Do they begin their search for information at the top by looking at industries they believe will be impacted favorably by consumer demand and trends in the economy and then look for stocks in those industries? If so, they're top-down investors.

*Bottom-up investors* tend to look at financial fundamentals first and compare them across companies and even industries to find those stocks whose numbers add up to what they believe will be a successful investment: strong annual growth rates (some money managers look for growth of upwards of 15% annually), efficient management, and the ability of a company to beat mainstream analysts' predictions about how well it will perform.

*Top-down investors* look for opportunities and the promise of growth in sectors or specialized areas of the economy such as autos, banks, computers, health care,

 **bottom-up investors**
those who use a stock-picking strategy based on a search for value using fundamentals; tends to work best in a bear market.

**top-down investors**
those who use a stock-picking strategy based on selection of growing and high growth potential stocks within sectors that are generally doing well; tends to work best in a bull market.

and technology. In the course of a *business cycle*, sectors come in and out of favor.

For instance, when interest rates decrease to a low enough level, literally hundreds of thousands of new buyers flood the real estate market. As a result, home resales boom and builders can barely keep up with the demand for new homes, as happened in the late 1990s. Investors watching the economy who want to invest in growing sectors decide housing would fit the bill—and then pick stocks within that sector. That's top-down investing.

Bottom-up investing starts from the ground up. Bottom-up investors tend to ignore the big picture, like what's going on in different sectors of the economy, so they can concentrate on individual company stories. In essence, with bottom-up investing you look for opportunity where you find it. For instance, the housing sector may be hurting next year if interest rates head up, but certain home builders such as Ryland Home may still be able to buck the trend by using innovation. Maybe Ryland has lower land costs, creates a popular housing model, or finds a successful marketing program that works with the middle class. If Ryland's numbers look sound it could easily go on the buy list of a bottom-up investor, despite the nosedive in new business the rest of the players in the housing sector might be suffering from as rising interest rates squeeze off demand.

Growth investors tend to be top-down, picking growing sectors first, then selecting stocks within those sectors that are growing and that show high growth potential for the future. Value investors, as you might expect from anyone hunting bargains, are bottom-up investors. The growth and success of sectors mean less to them than the fundamentals of individual companies if they believe a company has as yet undiscovered potential that will be a boon to its stock price somewhere in the near term.

You can embrace either system and do well over time. However, growth strategies work best in bull markets where a rising tide carries all boats. Value strategies shine in bear markets where there are more bargains to be found as the market gets battered and you're willing to buy low.

Before you swear allegiance to one or the other ap-

 **business cycle**
a regular and recurring cycle of accelerating business and profits within a sector, followed by that sector falling out of favor. The business cycle is a telling sign of where the country is economically—expansion, recovery, or recession.

proach, understand that many investors not only mix both styles of analysis, but gladly acknowledge doing so.

**Growth at a Reasonable Price.** This type of analysis, also known in the professional money management trade as *GARP*, acknowledges the weakness inherent in growth investing that can overtake some investors—namely, that it is possible for you to lose sight of some important facts and pay too much for shares of a stock that meet all or most of the other fundamental criteria you've established. There are no hard-and-fast GARP rules governing what growth should cost investors since stocks and their prices are so disparate. Instead, you must set your own reasonable price parameters.

The phenomenal rise of Internet stocks in the last half of the 1990s represents how willing some investors are to pay for growth at any price, firm in their belief that the U.S. stock market could continue its stellar growth. In the course of just four short months in 1998, investors may or may not have adhered to some form of GARP as they traded Internet offerings like eBay, the stock of the first online auctioneer, up from an *offering price* of $18 to more than $241 a share—a whopping increase of 1,240%.

As you consider your own comfort level and the individual stocks on your watch list, think about GARP and whether you believe the price of an individual company's shares can continue to rise. Think of GARP as a pragmatic buffer of sorts, designed to add a dose of realism to what can quickly become investing exuberance when the prices of the stocks in question seem to have no ceiling in sight.

### Technical Analysis

Many times investment prices rise and fall enough to create a pattern. *Technical analysis* attempts to capture that pattern as an indication of when to buy and sell a stock. It sounds drier than it is because it conjures up pictures of charts laden with data, but those who practice technical analysis are really trying to create a model they can use to help them decide when stock prices will rise and fall. Such technical models, when they do their job right, use

---

**GARP**
growth at a reasonable price—a type of analysis tempering growth investing with price parameters.

**offering price**
the price of a stock when it is first publicly offered in an IPO. This price can increase or decrease within minutes of the initial trade if it is traded again.

**technical analysis**
a type of stock analysis that tries to use patterns in investment prices to make decisions about when to buy and sell a stock; does not use fundamentals.

patterns of stock purchases to create predictions about future prices. A technical analyst focuses on the movements of stock prices in the past and present in the belief that they will shed light on the thinking of investors regarding the future value of a stock.

Financial fundamentals are irrelevant, technical analysts argue, because the market is already efficient. What that means, they believe, is that investors have already performed fundamental analysis on a stock, so there is little if any new information to be discovered. As a result, many ignore both the quality and source of information and focus instead on the behavior of stock prices and the volume of purchases.

Technical analysis doesn't track just any stock purchases; it tracks those made by big institutions, which drive much of the market's up-and-down movement. Often changes in volume are seen as a signal to buy or sell. In a perfect world, such analysis would be able to tell you when the price of a stock reaches it lowest or highest point. That way, you could buy low and sell high, like you're supposed to.

To make things a bit more complicated, some technical analysts are also contrarians. In other words, they believe that the mood in the market is usually wrong, and therefore do the opposite.

Here's a closer look at some of the indicators that technical analysts track:

• *Insider trading.* When a senior executive at a company or a major shareholder begins buying or selling shares, it is often seen as a signal that prices are about to climb or drop.

• *Investor confidence.* The idea is that the level of confidence being exhibited by investors influences price movements. One common notion is that increases or decreases in bond investments are one of the basic indicators of investor confidence. Increases in bond investments are supposed to signal decreasing investor confidence in the stock market, and vice versa.

• *Volume.* There is some belief that daily trading volume is an indicator of whether prices are going up or down.

**insider trading**
the buying or selling of a company's stock by senior executives or major shareholders; seen as a signal that prices will change.

**investor confidence**
the level of assurance being exhibited by investors, which can influence price movements.

**volume**
the total number of shares traded on an exchange in a given period. Believed by some to indicate whether prices will go up or down.

High volume during a price increase is seen as an indicator of bull market conditions. High volume during price declines is seen as bearish. While volume tended to increase gradually before significant price declines in the past, the long-running bull market of the 1990s turned this indicator on its ear.

**mutual fund indicators**
the amount of money in mutual fund portfolios held in cash. Can be seen as an indicator of future big stock purchases (driving up prices), or stagnancy, letting prices decrease.

• *Mutual fund indicators.* With more than $5 trillion in assets, mutual funds exert a lot of buying power. When funds have a good deal of cash in their portfolios, it can be seen as a signal that they'll have to make stock purchases at some point in the near future and those purchases will drive up prices. At the other end of the spectrum, when funds are fully invested in the stock and bond markets, it can be seen as a signal that prices have no place left to go but down.

But technical analysis has its shortcomings. Repeated studies to see if technical analysis predicted stock price movements have been inconclusive. (*A Random Walk Down Wall Street*, by Burton G. Malkiel, on the reading list in Chapter 16, details much of this research.)

Many chartists, as technical analysts are often called, use this style of analysis in conjunction with fundamental and *quantitative analysis.* Taken together the three analysis styles should ideally be used as a way to narrow the field of potential stock winners.

**quantitative analysis**
a type of stock analysis relying solely on quantitative, mathematical methods of searching for opportunity.

### Quantitative Analysis

These are the true numbers people. They have almost no interest in a company's underlying business, but instead search for opportunity using a quantitative, mathematical approach. These investors view fundamental analysis as speculation. The founder of much of what quants believe is Benjamin Graham, who, when he was running the Graham-Newman Partnership, told his analysts not to talk to the managers at companies whose stocks they were interested in buying because it would only be a distraction.

Most quants use computer screens to find investments. These screens sort stocks using various factors, which might include finding those stocks that have exhibited a certain growth rate, strong sales, and high-volume trading. Then they deliver a list of potential investments that fit the criteria quant managers have designated. Powerful computers and personal computers (PCs) have increased the popularity of quantitative analysis. Indeed, it finds its way into plenty of other investment styles because it can help narrow the field to the best candidates.

You'll hear relative strength discussed often among quants. It is a way to measure a company's performance against the overall market and can be used to compare a stock to its competitors.

## Day Trading

*Day traders* buy stocks or other financial instruments and then sell them in the course of the day or even a few hours. They attempt to make money as a result of minute movements in share prices, a practice that can require many, many trades. The number of day traders has increased in recent years as the stock market has soared. If you invest online, you may be sorely tempted to trade early and often. After all, commissions are low, information is current, and you know what you're doing. While someday you may join the ranks of professional traders who move millions in the course of a day, for now you should consider yourself a buy-and-hold kind of investor who makes long-term decisions.

 **day traders** those who buy financial instruments and then sell them in the course of a day, attempting to profit from minute market fluctuations.

### What Style Investor Are You?

Much of your success as an investor is linked to your style. To help you understand how you will react in a variety of investment situations and how those reactions may impact your success, Moneymax Profiling System was developed by the Financial Psychology Corporation of Reno, Nevada. You can find it for free at the Mutual Fund Education Alliance web site (www.mfea.com). The test sorts investors into nine money personalities. Choose the one that character-

*(Continued)*

izes your own money management style to see where
your strengths and weaknesses lie.

**Money Masters.** Money masters are very involved in managing their investments and value
sound advice. They are the number one wealth accu-
mulators, and, though they may not necessarily be
the biggest wage earners in a company or neighbor-
hood, they are diligent and determined.

**Safety Players.** These investors lack the confidence necessary to take calculated investment risks,
even after training. Consequently, they value security above all, and tend to find one or two strategies
and repeat them over and over, regardless of success
or failure.

**Entrepreneurs.** These high-income, mostly male
investors favor investing in stocks and get a kick
from the power and prestige successful stock picks
bring them both in and out of the office. They're
most likely to boast about or even exaggerate their
stock-picking prowess.

**Optimists.** These investors seek peace of mind
and use money to gain it. They're more likely to invest quickly, almost as if they want to get it over
with, rather than invest for the long term.

**Hunters.** Mostly women, these investors trust
luck and make impulsive investment decisions
based on gut reaction. They tend, however, to be
highly educated and have above-average incomes.

**Perfectionists.** To avoid making mistakes this
group also avoids making decisions. They consequently struggle to find appropriate investments
and may leave money sitting in cash or cash equiv-

alents for long periods of time as a result of paralysis.

**Achievers.** These family-oriented investors value their own hard work and want to manage their money themselves. Preserving assets is their priority, beyond transforming their money into untold wealth. They may tend to play it overly safe for their age and investment time horizon.

**Producers.** These people are worker bees, who rank high in work ethic but low in income. While their hearts are in the right place, they lack confidence in their ability to invest. Happily, they do respond to financial education.

**High Rollers.** Call them thrill seekers, because these investors enjoy taking risks with their money. When they win, everybody knows it. When they lose, they tend to lose big.

Once you've determined your investment style, use it to help refine your investment plan and overcome weaknesses. For example, achievers may want to add more growth-oriented investments that will help them meet their goals over the long term and serve to offset their tendency to opt for conservative investments that preserve capital. High rollers, mindful of their taste for risk, might build more diversification into their portfolios to compensate for the thrill they get from the chase of above-average investment returns. This high-rolling investment style assumes above-average risk, which diversification will allow high rollers to offset.

# Chapter 6

# How Performance Is Measured

The world of investment performance is dotted with benchmarks, landmarks, ratios, and factors. You can measure investment performance in a dozen ways, then compare what you've measured with everything else you've measured. That will give you an understanding of how well the stock, bond, or mutual fund you've selected is performing compared with its peers, however you've defined them.

This process, however tedious it might seem, gives you perspective. It allows you to compare and contrast a variety of performance measures to ensure you're getting what you think you're getting and getting what you want—before you sink your money into an investment. You may find in your analysis of the measures you collect that the investment you thought you wanted isn't the one you really want at all. But by comparing and contrasting similar investments, you'll have a much clearer understanding of what you're looking for and looking at. By examining the universe of like investments—for instance, mutual funds that invest in the financial services arena—you'll get a sense of not only which do well and which do poorly, but why. At the same time, you'll find it easier to take the information you've collected and the judgments you've made, and make predictions or *projections* about future performance.

**projection**
an estimate of how well an investment is likely to perform that is based on performance comparisons, analysis, and performance of the sector and economy as a whole.

Even if you end up casting aside the original invest-ment you were interested in as a result of your roundup of performance measures, going through the drill will give you a selection of investments to choose from and a broad perspective of what is going on in particular industries and the investment markets overall. You'll invest with your eyes wide open, knowing the potential benefits and rewards of any investment you make, along with its draw-backs and risk. Consider this chapter, then, a primer on performance measures for mutual funds, stocks, and bonds. We'll discuss easy ways you can find this informa-tion in later chapters. For now, let's concentrate on what is being measured.

## MUTUAL FUND PERFORMANCE

As you begin to winnow down the mutual funds you're interested in, here is the performance information you want to find and compare. Don't forget, too, that a fund's performance is an amalgamation of the total performance of its underlying assets. If it invests in stocks, bonds or a combination of both, you'll get the total return of those assets, not just the good performance.

That's important to keep in mind if your aim is to build a portfolio of different or diversified mutual funds. Sometimes investors are tempted to put all of their money in the hottest-performing funds at the moment. As we write this, the funds with the best returns were science and technology funds, with a 11.28% total return for Jan-uary 1999. That compared favorably to 0.13% total return for growth and income funds. But the problem with con-centrating your investments in the hottest sector of the markets and the economy is this: Just as all of these funds are top performers today, it's a pretty sure bet that most of them will pretty much drop off the charts in the foresee-able future.

While you want some representation of the hottest sector, it should be just one part of a diversified portfolio and surely no more than 20%.

### Fund Measurements

**Net Asset Value.** This is the price per share of a mutual fund. It's called the fund's NAV for short and is how mutual funds are priced. Each trading day, the total market value of the securities (stocks, bonds, etc.) the fund owns are added up. Fund managers (or accountants) then deduct all of the fund's liabilities and any fees it owes to come up with its NAV. Why think about NAV? Because share pricing is as important with mutual funds as it is with stocks. You want to buy low, not high. If you buy high the value of the fund has nowhere to go to come up with the gains you're expecting. To distinguish high from low when it comes to NAV, call the fund company and ask for a prospectus or go online to the fund's web site. This will give you a historical perspective of a fund's price, so you can see the peaks and valleys.

**Total Return.** The *total return* number is important because it tells you what a fund's bottom line is—what it charges you in expenses, what it pays out in distributions, and what you have earned by investing in the fund. You can find funds' total returns in the *Wall Street Journal's* Mutual Funds Monthly Review, which it publishes the first business day of each month, and in *Investor's Business Daily*, the widely available newspaper for investors. Personal finance magazines such as *Kiplinger's* and *SmartMoney* also provide total returns for the funds it reviews. This number is a good tool to use for comparison shopping.

**Year-to-Date Return.** *Year-to-date return* tells you how much a fund has earned so far this year, which is a good indication of how well the investments it selected—or at least the type of investments it selected—are doing. For much of the 1990s, since blue-chip stocks dominated the market, it was difficult for blue-chip stock fund managers not to do well. You can also use this measurement to compare funds, but it's not as telling as total return since expenses and distributions aren't deducted.

**Annualized Returns.** *One-, three-, and five-year annualized returns* give you a perspective on the fund and fund

**total return**
a measure of a fund's total return to the investor, taking charges, dividends, and earnings into account.

**year-to-date return**
how much a fund has earned so far this year.

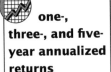
**one-, three-, and five-year annualized returns**
a measure of the earnings of a fund over the past one, three, or five years, which gives you an idea of how performance has held up over time.

manager's historical performance and how performance has held up over time. These numbers provide no guarantee really of how a fund will perform in the future. But they do give you some sense of how well the fund has fared over time compared to similar funds, how much volatility there has been, and whether the fund has hit some rough patches.

**Annual Expenses.** The *annual expenses* fee is a percentage of your investment that the fund charges you every year to cover its overhead and administrative charges including salaries. The fee does not include the commissions you pay to buy a particular fund.

**Maximum Initial Sales Charges, Commissions, or Loads.** By any name, this is what you pay to have a mutual fund sold to you. You won't pay anything for no-load mutual fund shares if you buy them directly from the company. But if you choose to buy a fund from a broker, the *maximum initial sales charges, commissions, or loads* tells you the largest possible percentage of your money that a broker, financial planner, insurance agent, or even an accountant who sells mutual funds will get to pocket. Commissions, also called loads, can range as high as 5.75%. If you're willing to pay one, deduct it from the amount you're investing and shave the percentage from any performance you get the first year. That means if a fund earns 12.75% and you paid a 5.75% load or commission, you actually earned only 7%. That's worth thinking about long and hard.

**Underlying Fund Investments.** Take a look at a fund's quarterly report, or at least its *prospectus*, to see what its actual investments are. Stick with the top five investments if that makes it easier. You're not trying to judge whether these stocks or bonds are great performers necessarily (that's why you're investing in a mutual fund—you expect the fund manager to do that for you), but you do want to make sure that the funds you're buying are not all duplicating the same portfolio of investments. "I can't tell you how many investors have come to me with a portfolio

 **annual expenses** the percentage of your investment that a mutual fund charges every year to cover its overhead and administrative charges including salaries.

 **maximum initial sales charges, commissions, or loads** fees you pay to have a mutual fund sold to you. They can range as high as 5.75%.

 **prospectus** a printed statement describing a fund that is distributed to prospective investors.

**concentration**
a lack of diver-
sification in a
collection of
investments,
which increases
risk.

**portfolio
turnover**
the amount of
buying and sell-
ing a mutual fund
manager does,
which affects
both expenses
and returns.

**standard
deviation**
how much an
investment goes
up and down in
price in a fixed
time period; a
numeric measure
of volatility.
Higher standard
deviation repre-
sents higher
volatility or risk.

of 10 mutual funds that essentially owned all the same stocks," says Mary K. Sullivan, a financial planner in San Francisco. If that's the case, no matter how great the performance, you'll end up with *concentration*; and when that sector falls out of favor, and they always do, your overall portfolio will take a nosedive.

**Annual Portfolio Turnover.** This is how often a fund manager sells stocks. A *portfolio turnover* rate of about 85%—the average for large-cap growth stock funds—means that each year on average a fund manager sells 85% of the stocks he or she buys. Funds with low turnover rates may have better performance since they do not have to pay the commissions for trading stocks frequently. While you won't find these costs added to your annual expenses fee, you'll feel them in lower returns.

**Standard Deviation.** This is the true expression of a fund's volatility, or how much its performance bounces around either year-to-year or month-to-month, depending on what source of information you're using. It doesn't matter which you use, but make sure when you're making comparisons to be consistent. In general, the higher a fund's *standard deviation*, the more you stand to lose in a volatile or down market.

## STOCK NUMBERS AND BEYOND

For strict technical and quantitative types, everything they need and want can be found in performance numbers. They buy on the numbers and sell on the numbers. They believe that by looking at certain measures they can predict that a stock price is going to rise and get in for the ride.

In contrast, the mantra for fundamental and qualitative analysts might best be summarized this way: Companies don't create just statistics, they make shoes, and toothpaste, and computers. How well they do these things determines whether they make money or not and whether they stay in business or close. If you're looking for qualitative measures of a company's abilities and potential for success, you measure performance, to be sure, but you also train an eye on management, sales, and market penetration before you make a final decision.

## A Closer Look at Stock Performance

As you begin to investigate companies, you'll soon discover your own interest in and tolerance for numbers. To help you find what you need to look for, here are the most often used measures of company success, which can be found in a company's balance sheet, income statement, and cash flow summaries. These measures are generally understood to be meaningful indications of performance, so you should understand them before you begin your research into which companies to buy and which to avoid.

**Book Value per Share.** This is one of the most under-appreciated measures of a company's success. Book value per share is calculated by dividing tangible *book value* by the number of outstanding shares. In some cases book value can be significantly more or less than the current market value of a stock. That means you might be able to buy a stock at below its book value or you might have to pay a premium. The point is, book value is not representative of the market's perception of a company's value.

 **book value**
how much a company would be worth if it liquidated all of its assets and paid off all of its debt tomorrow.

What it represents is the baseline of a company's worth, and what you would get if it had to liquidate all of its assets and pay off all its debts tomorrow. What's left over would be its book value per share. If a stock's market value is $35 and its book value is $26, then in the worst of scenarios, such as bankruptcy, you could lose $9 a share. Can you live with that?

If a stock is trading at more than its book value, it is trading at a premium. That means the market thinks it's worth more than the total of its net assets. If a stock is trading at less than its book value, you have to figure out why. Has it been trading at less than book value since it was introduced? Or has its price taken a nosedive recently for some short-term reason? Unless you can answer these questions, move on to the next stock on your watch list.

"We don't buy cheap just to buy cheap," says Kathy

O'Connor, a comanager of the Eclipse Equity Fund. "Sometimes companies are cheap for good reason. We look for relative goodness, which we hope translates into positive reporting results for the companies."

**Dividends Paid.** Companies use dividends to distribute net profits to shareholders. In fact, dividends can represent a good percentage of the total return you earn as an investor. While the amount that is actually paid to an investor per 100 shares might be small, whether a company pays dividends or not constitutes a trend, and dividend trends are important.

Wall Street analysts often attach a significant degree of importance to whether a company issues a dividend and whether it matches or increases its dividend every year. Companies that can do this use it as a selling point. As a result, there is a great amount of pressure on companies to declare a dividend, even in years when they are strapped. Skipping one, however, can be the prudent thing to do, which is something you should bear in mind when examining a company's dividend history.

As you've already learned, companies that focus on growth do not pay dividends to their shareholders, but reinvest the funds instead as a means to continue growing. They contend that future growth is more important than current dividend payments.

How important are dividends to you? Are you investing for growth or income? If you're investing for growth, you want companies where management will reinvest profits. On the other hand, if you need income, find companies that pay high ones even if it's at the expense of investing in lines of business and strategies that could buy current and future price appreciation.

**earnings per share (EPS)**
net profits of a company during a specified time period, divided by the number of outstanding common shares during that period.

**net profits**
the profits of a company after taxes, preferred shareholders, and bondholders are paid.

**Earnings per Share.** This is the definitive measure of performance for most investors because it can represent a fairly accurate picture of how well a company has performed in its ability to create earnings for investors.

*Earnings per share (EPS)* is determined by dividing net profits by the average number of common shares outstanding during the period being measured. *Net profits* are calculated after paying taxes and preferred shareholders and bondholders. Investors use EPS to compare year-to-year performance. A stock's earnings per share trend can be an important indicator that will allow you to judge growth over many years. If growth is consistent, it indicates that a company is adept at creating and managing controlled growth. See a more inconsistent, even erratic pattern? Some stocks can show both earnings and losses over time, making it very difficult to predict any long-term growth pattern.

Unless you're investing play money, look for earnings growth that has lasted over a period of at least five years. More aggressive investors look for earnings growth averaging 20% or more over that period, but slower, steady growth is perfectly acceptable, too. As a rule of thumb, larger, solid companies tend to reinvest 35% or more of their profits in the expansion of their business, so their earnings growth won't be as spectacular. The rest goes to pay dividends to shareholders.

While increases in earnings are obviously positive, most companies tend to have a natural ceiling on the amount of growth investors might be able to expect. An expectation that earnings growth will continue after periods of significant growth may be unrealistic.

Of equal importance to these "trailing earnings" figures are projections of future earnings growth. These future projections are usually the handiwork of analysts who work for brokerage houses, mutual funds, and other companies. Why is it important to consider future earnings growth? Because these predictions, again determined by dividing estimated future net income by the number of shares outstanding, can have an enormous impact on stock prices. That's because they show the possible rate of future growth or decline compared to current and past growth or decline.

## *Are There Ongoing Earnings?*

When you are checking out earnings be certain you are examining earnings that were generated by routine business operations and not those from nonrecurring situations. Companies selling off subsidiaries can look highly profitable until you realize the money came from onetime sales of major assets, and not from routine business. A company can also undertake a financial strategy, such as buying back large blocks of its common stock, which can increase share prices even if profits are declining. Conversely, a company can look like it is in trouble when its earnings (or lack of them) reflect a onetime loss, say from a lawsuit.

**cash flow**
the amount of net cash generated by a business during a specific time, taking expenses such as depreciation into account.

**Cash Flow.** *Cash flow* is another leading indicator of performance, one many analysts believe is even more important than P/E (discussed next) because it is less easy to manipulate. It is the amount of *net* cash generated by a business, calculated by adding charges like depreciation to the net income, which is the profit a company makes after taxes are paid.

Analysts consider it so important because it is the fuel, in essence, that drives the company. Without positive cash flow, it is more difficult to improve performance. Large amounts of cash flow, however, make companies tempting takeover targets. That's because the money can be used to pay for part or all of the takeover.

**Price-Earnings Ratio (P/E).** This measure tells you the relationship between a stock's price and the company's earnings for the past year. It will help you keep the stock's price and its earnings potential in mind. After all, you don't want to pay too high a price for a company whose earnings don't warrant the expense.

To find a company's P/E ratio, take the current price of a share of stock and divide it by current earnings per share. The result is the stock's price-earnings ratio. Typical P/Es range from 8 to 10 times annual earnings, which are common P/Es among auto company stocks. But P/Es can go as high as 50 times earnings or even higher for high-flying high-tech stocks whose share prices typically outstrip their earnings by a wide margin. Some P/Es rise above 100, though they don't often stay there. Companies with stock prices far ahead of the underlying value of shares can only disappoint Wall Street with lower-than-expected earnings or the failure of a new product. That tends to bring lofty valuations, or stock prices, down to earth fast.

And that's the key reason to measure P/E. It is the most common way to measure the price of a stock relative to the market, relative to the industry sector in which it does business, and relative to a company's own past performance. You can also think of P/E ratios as a measure of the willingness of investors to pay for the potential of future gain. Stocks with P/Es above their benchmark, typically the S&P 500 Index, are said to trade at a premium to the market. Those with P/Es below their benchmark are trading at a discount. Stocks with high P/Es tend to have higher earnings growth rates. Those with lower P/Es tend to have slower earnings growth rates. *Income stocks* would fall in this latter category. Of course, income stocks offer higher dividends, for those investors who need them, rather than price appreciation, so you wouldn't expect them to have high P/Es. Utility companies such as electric, gas, and telephone companies are examples of income stocks.

 **income stocks**
stocks that offer higher dividends rather than higher earnings growth rates, such as utility companies.

Ideally, what you're looking for with growth stocks is a high earnings growth rate and a lower-than-average P/E ratio. For instance, if XYZ Internet Inc.'s profits are growing at 18% a year and its P/E ratio is less than 18, the stock might be a bargain because its price hasn't caught up with its earnings potential yet.

Carmakers are in a cyclical business, and their performance is often closely tied to the U.S. economy's performance—up for a few years, down for a few more. There's no reason to pay a premium for them. High-tech companies seem, at least in the late 1990s, to own the future. Investors are willing to pay a premium of many times earnings for Cisco Systems, the giant networking company, because its potential appears to be so great. The stock bounced back from $40 a share in October 1998, where it had nosedived to when the Justice Department accused Cisco managers of anticompetitive activities, to more than $120 a share in January 1999.

Low-P/E stocks—those below the Dow Jones Industrials or the S&P 500 Index—are not a lost cause by any means, however. Just ask anyone who bought Ford stock in 1996 and saw the investment double and then some in just a few years. Low-P/E stocks are sometimes considered underpriced or value stocks and potentially a bargain with a brighter future. The trick, of course, is knowing when a dog of a stock is about to shed its flea-bitten hide and turn into a value stock. Analysts often call a stock's P/E the "multiple" and use it in this context: "It has a multiple of 24 and trades at a premium to the market."

In addition to comparing stocks to an index to measure their relative value, investors also compare P/Es to the sector in which a company operates. This is a way to further define the relative value of an investment. For example, an automaker with a P/E of 12 might be considered undervalued compared to the S&P 500, but auto stocks historically trade below the market. In this case, 12 would be considered slightly high for a P/E and would likely make the stock a less attractive investment.

Note that P/Es can be inflated artificially if a company had a bad year and shows low earnings as a result, thus making for what analysts call "easy comparisons." That is, the price of the stock has risen, to be sure, but with earnings low, the resulting P/E will be artificially high.

**price-to-sales ratio**
the price of a stock divided by its sales per share.

**Price-to-Sales Ratio.** This ratio compares a company's stock price to its sales per share. A low *price-to-sales ratio* indicates an undervalued stock, but one with the potential to grow in value because the sales are there. Only the profit margin has to be improved for the shares to rise in value. A high price-to-sales ratio can indicate a stock that is overvalued.

### New World Order

In the late 1990s, other stock picking measurements began to come into vogue. Since the price-earnings ratios for some stocks such as America Online, Amazon.com, Dell Computer, and Yahoo! made them look incredibly expensive, while the stocks continued to grow anyway, stock pickers began to find different measures more meaningful, including gross margins of above 60% or so (Microsoft's, for instance, was 92% at the end of 1998), net margins of above 10% (Microsoft's was 30%), and cash-to-debt ratios of 1.5% or better (Microsoft had $18 billion in assets, no debt).

In the new world order where many are seeking to value supposedly overpriced stocks, analysts have also begun looking at *flow ratio* (which is a company's current assets minus all the cash, divided by current liabilities), which they say tells them how well a company is being managed and whether managers are efficient at moving product out the door and getting paid for it. Flow ratios of less than 1% are considered good. For instance, Dell Computer had a flow ratio of 0.78% at the end of 1998.

Valuing certain stocks, especially technology stocks, can be difficult at times, admits Kevin Landis, a mutual fund manager with Firsthand Funds, who manages several of the company's high-tech offerings. "It isn't like picking the best carmaker," Landis says. "These are new industries creating new technologies and products where the demand can be virtually unknown." The idea behind embracing the unknown is to do it in sync with your overall goals, risk tolerance, and investment time horizon—not by making a huge sector bet that is far too risky.

**flow ratio**
a company's current assets minus cash, divided by current liabilities. Flow ratios of less than 1% are considered good.

## BOND PERFORMANCE

Bonds are a whole different beast than stocks. While it's a good idea to look at historical performance when buying bonds, their current performance is usually very closely tied to current interest rates (*inverse correlation*). That's why the following principle is the one to remember when buying bonds or bond funds. When interest rates go up, bond prices go down. And when interest rates go down, bond prices go up.

Typically the longer the term (length of maturity) of a bond, the higher the rate you will earn. After all, if you're lending money to a corporation, a municipality, or the government for a longer period of time, you'll want to be compensated for that with a higher rate. At the same time, however, the longer the maturity, the higher the

**inverse correlation**
a relationship between two measures in which an increase in the first tends to coincide with a decrease in the second. Bond prices and interest rates are inversely correlated.

**discount**
the amount
below its face
value that a bond
is selling at.

**basis
point**
one-hundredth of
a percent; a unit
in which interest
rates are mea-
sured.

**annual
interest**
the interest you
earn in one year
on an invest-
ment. On a bond,
annual interest
equals the
coupon rate mul-
tiplied by the
face value.

**current
yield**
the annual inter-
est on a bond
divided by its
market value and
multiplied by
100.

risk. For instance, if you buy a long-term government bond and interest rates go up and you have to sell, you'll have to accept less than what you paid—that is, less than the face value of the bond.

Say you buy a 20-year corporate bond with a face value of $1,000 paying a 6% yield. For that you'll get $60 a year in interest over the next 20 years. But let's say for some reason five years from now you need to cash in the bond. Now, in a rising interest rate environment, similar bonds are paying 10%. As a result, you won't be able to sell your bond for the full face value; you'll have to sell it at a *discount*.

In common parlance, if rates are rising you would not want to tie your money up in a 20- or 30-year bond because you could lose out on both the higher interest rate and large interest payments you'd be able to get at some point in the foreseeable future as a result.

## Bond Measurements

**Basis Points.** Interest rates are represented as *basis points*. For instance, 100 basis points equal 1%, and 10 basis points equal 0.1%. For every basis point that the interest rate goes up or down, the discount rate goes up or down one hundredth of a percent.

**Discount.** The discount is the amount below its face value that a bond is selling at. If you buy a bond at a price of 90, you're buying it at 10% below its face value.

**Coupon Rate.** This is the amount of interest that is paid. Coupon rates can be either fixed rate, where you are paid the same amount of interest every year, or floating rate, where interest payments are adjusted periodically based on the movements of a predetermined index.

**Annual Interest.** The *annual interest* on a bond can be determined by multiplying the coupon rate by the face value.

**Current Yield.** The *current yield* is the annual interest payment of the bond divided by the total market value of the bond (or the current market value if the price has changed) and then multiplying by 100 to get a percentage. If annual interest payments are $90, you would divide that amount by the total market value, say $1,000, and then multiply the result by 100 to get the current yield, which in this case would be 9%. Since market prices fluctuate daily, current yields will change frequently.

**Yield to Maturity.** As you already know, every bond has a maturity date. At the same time, you receive interest payments annually or semiannually until the bond matures. The *yield to maturity* is the total of interest payments you can expect to earn if you hold the bond until maturity, plus a bond's coupon rate, current market price, and the years left until the bond matures. The calculation can be tricky, so have whomever you're buying the bond from provide it, whether it's the Treasury Department, a corporation, a municipality, or a broker. The yield to maturity is essential to obtain, since it is a bond's total return.

**yield to maturity**
a bond's total return.

**Highs, Lows, and Closing Prices.** This gives you the high, low and closing prices of bonds for the previous trading day.

**Net Change.** *Net change* represents the difference in price from the previous day's trading activity.

**net change**
the difference between an investment's price yesterday and today.

**Ratings.** You want the bond you're buying to have a rating of A or above from rating companies such as Moody's Investors Service, Standard & Poor's, and Fitch's Investment Service. Bonds with ratings lower than this pay higher yields, but not high enough to take on the attendant risk. You can earn more with less risk by using stocks. Higher ratings are a good way of ensuring that whomever you're lending money to—which is essentially what you do when you buy a bond—will be around to pay you back and not have to declare bankruptcy. In essence, the ratings show the bond issuers' credit risk.

*Chapter*

# The Great Benchmarks of Market Performance

As we write this, the Dow Jones Industrial Average has slipped to 10,951, dropping more than 44 points. Nasdaq has risen to 2,756, up 24.09 points. And Standard & Poor's 500 has climbed to 1,379, inching up 1.93 points. If you don't know what these indexes are, you soon will. And when you do, you'll be able to assess how well the stock market we were in compares to the one you're in as you read this.

An index is a statistical yardstick or gauge of a particular market based on the average prices or price movement of a group of like investments, such as small- or large-cap stocks or corporate bonds. An index can also measure other types of data, such as the consumer price index (CPI).

The important point to remember, regardless of which type of investments you're measuring performance for, is that all investment performance is relative. What happened five years ago is incidental today. Bragging rights for an annual return of 10% might be considerable in the midst of a recession, but that kind of performance would surely be viewed as less than stellar in a raging bull market like the one investors rode throughout the 1990s. The trick is being able to tell definitively how well the performances of your invest-

98

ments stack up against those of their peers in the market you're in. Once you do that you'll be able to answer questions like: Is this stock's performance average? Is this mutual fund's performance well above average? Is this bond's performance poor? Soon you'll be able to answer these questions using indexes. Remember, however, that average performance isn't necessarily a bad thing in investing. After all, our investment choices make up the average. In some periods—1995 to 1997 was one such period—under 7% of money managers beat the average. So don't fret too much if any of your investments are turning in average performance.

Knowing your indexes is also a tool you can use for reading the market—determining whether the stock, bond, and mutual fund markets appear to be headed up, down, or at least into more volatile water. Attempting to gauge the direction of the market you're investing in is important because you want to buy low, not at a market's peak. If you buy at the very crest of an investment's performance, your investment has no place to go but down. Of course, no one can tell you how high a market can climb or to what depths it might plummet. And no one can tell you when. But by watching a particular index, you'll get a sense about whether a specific market—say large-cap stocks—seems to be headed into a free fall, is overheated, or is zipping along nicely, based on what it's been doing for days, weeks, or even months or years.

There are dozens of benchmarks, generally indexes, against which you can compare all or part of your portfolio's record. The Russell 2000, the Wilshire 5000, 30-year Treasury rates, and the price of an ounce of gold are all benchmarks investors use to gauge the success of their investments and general market direction.

Some indexes are based on mathematical computations that yield a factor—a number that captures a group of investments' prices or their price movement up or down. Other indexes, like gold, merely reflect the average price of the commodity. Still others reflect movement in an interest rate, like 30-year Treasuries, which benchmarks the safest of all investments.

## WANT TO BUY 500 STOCKS FOR $100 A MONTH?

There is another way to use an index, and that is to spread your money among its underlying investments in an attempt to duplicate their average performance. Sound odd?

It's likely that none of us would want to pay the hefty commissions it would cost us to buy all of the investments in an index. For instance, purchasing even the top 100 stocks in the Russell 2000, an index of small-cap growth stocks, would cost an investor a whopping $1,400 in commissions alone, even if he or she used a deeply discounted brokerage service. Not surprisingly, that money would be far better off invested. So what are your alternatives if you want your own portfolio to track the performance of an index?

Try an index mutual fund. These mutual funds do what most investors can't do: They buy all of the stocks or bonds in an index. There are many advantages to index fund investing. First, index funds tend to maximize performance over time, not least because they minimize fees. They're not actively traded portfolios, so the cost of the portfolio turnover associated with *active management* is minimized.

There are two costs managers incur as a result of high portfolio turnover. They have to pay brokerage commissions each time they buy or sell a security, eating into profits. Also, if the securities have appreciated in price, the fund's investors will get hit with capital gains taxes that will accrue until you sell the investment; then you'll have to pay the taxes. As a result, low turnover is desirable in a mutual fund.

On average, active mutual funds cost investors about 1.5% in regular expenses and another 1% in trading costs to buy and sell stocks. That gives active mutual fund managers a 2.5% handicap right out of the box. Active management is the opposite of index investing (also known as passive management), which requires that you invest in the securities chosen for you by the people who run the index.

**active management**
a style of mutual fund management in which managers continually select securities to buy and sell, as opposed to the passive style used in managing an index fund, in which the securities that make up an index are

Another reason index mutual funds are attractive is because they hold fund managers to a certain investment philosophy or discipline. When held to a discipline, managers cannot make wild judgment calls or allow their investment style to drift into an area not foreseen or desired by investors. Why does it matter? Well, if you choose a value mutual fund because you want exposure to undervalued stocks, you do not want the manager to start accumulating growth and blue-chip stocks. That would mean he or she were guilty of *style drift.*

The problem with style drift is shown in this example: Two mutual funds you had bought because of their different objectives both suddenly start buying up small-cap stocks. You had bought one fund because you wanted dividends, and you know small caps rarely pay dividends. You'll be getting twice as much exposure to more volatile growth now, instead of some of the income you were counting on. In addition, if you were counting on one type of fund to offset risk in another, that safety net will be eliminated if a fund manager drifts far enough away from his or her stated style.

With index mutual fund investing you also get a certain degree of predictability. You can count on the fund to do just about what the index does—and just about what the underlying market it is measuring does.

If someone captures the movement of some type of market in an index, chances are there is a mutual fund that invests in the investments in the index. You can go as plain-vanilla as a Dow Jones Industrial Average index fund, which invests in the 30 blue-chip stocks that index represents. Or try something more exotic like a fund that invests in the stocks or bonds in a global market index such as the Morgan Stanley Capital International Index.

Which index fund should you invest in? That's something you have to decide by determining which index best fits into your overall portfolio, goals, and risk tolerance. Almost every mutual fund family has several index funds to choose from. Vanguard is the leader in creating index funds, but other large fund families like T. Rowe Price and Fidelity have index funds as well.

**style drift**
a change in the investment style of a mutual fund manager, causing the investments in the fund's portfolio to work against the fund's objective.

## WHICH INDEX IS WHICH?

Before you decide which index best measures the performance of your investments or which index's performance you would like to attempt to duplicate by investing in a comparable index mutual fund, you have to understand what one measures. Here are descriptions of many of the major indexes, along with explanations of what they measure and how.

## THE S&P 500

**S&P 500**
the index that represents the benchmark against which most money managers gauge their performance. Nine out of 10 fund managers don't outperform this index in any given five-year period.

For many investors, even professional money managers, this is the index that stands above the others as the measure of how you did. Sure, the Dow Jones Industrial Average gets headlines, but in reality it is more of a psychological gauge of investor sentiment about the stock market than it is a true measure of how a buck is faring in the investment marketplace. It is the *S&P 500* index that is the benchmark against which the performance of most portfolios is measured. About 97% of money managers and pension plan managers say they use the S&P 500 as part of their investing strategy. Companies on the index, which include giants such as RJR Nabisco, Honeywell, and Raytheon, have some $700 billion in outstanding stock.

The S&P 500 is so pervasive a benchmark that it is often used even when it is not the most appropriate of standards for measuring an investment's performance. A bond fund manager, for instance, would much rather you measured his or her fund's gain or loss against the Merrill Lynch bond index, which assesses how well the corporate bond market is doing overall. An investor with a portfolio of small-cap stocks would get a better picture of his or her assets by comparing them to the S&P Small Cap 600 index or the Russell 2000, which measure how the small-cap stock market is faring.

But fortunately or unfortunately, the performance of most mutual funds and stocks will be compared against the S&P 500. While historically large-cap stocks have re-turned about 10% a year, the past decade has seen returns exceed that number in every year except three (see Table 7.1). The stocks in the index sustained losses in only one year, 1990, but coming as it did between two years that produced 30% returns, this down year didn't pain in-vestors too much.

Like it or not, the press and investors tend to use the S&P 500 as the benchmark against which they mea-sure performance, so money managers don't have much choice but to take the challenge and try to beat this in-dex. Outperforming this index is perceived as a notewor-thy accomplishment—so much so that when a mutual fund manager does trounce it, you'll read it in news sto-ries about the hottest funds to own and in the fund's own advertisements. The task, however, is not an easy one. In fact, it's so daunting that 9 out of 10 mutual fund man-agers don't outperform the S&P 500 in any given five-year period. Obviously the ones who do get all of the attention and attract more investor dollars. But it's a diffi-cult achievement to maintain. Just because a manager or an individual stock outperformed the S&P 500 this year doesn't mean they'll do it again next year.

| TABLE 7.1 The S&P 500—Annualized Returns for the Past 10 Years | |
|---|---|
| Year | Return |
| 1989 | 31.69% |
| 1990 | –3.10% |
| 1991 | 30.47% |
| 1992 | 7.62% |
| 1993 | 10.08% |
| 1994 | 1.32% |
| 1995 | 37.58% |
| 1996 | 22.96% |
| 1997 | 33.36% |
| 1998 | 28.58% |

## The One to Beat

What is it with the S&P 500 that makes beating it such a daunting task? Its origins don't reveal the reasons for its pervasive influence. It was created in its current form in 1958 when to broaden an index's appeal, Standard & Poor's executives decided to expand what had been a 90-stock index into a benchmark of 500 stocks. The credit rating company then used the stock prices recorded in 1942–1943 as the base benchmark against which subsequent performance has been measured.

The 500 stocks are selected by a committee appointed by S&P executives and include 400 industrial companies, 40 utilities, 20 transportation companies, and 40 financial firms. The selection committee reviews the list periodically. As a result, up to 30 companies a year are replaced for any number of reasons. Reasons to get taken out of the index? Maybe a company shrank in size so it can no longer be considered a large-cap stock. Merging with or being acquired by a different type of company or declaring bankruptcy are also reasons to be removed from the index. S&P says that such companies and their performance are taken out of the index because they would throw off the average in a way that would make it a less meaningful benchmark.

The prices of shares in these 500 stocks are run through a computer model to yield a "factor" or measure of performance. That's the number you see reported in the newspaper or on the evening news along with the Dow Jones Industrial Average. You'll hear reports such as: "The S&P rose 3%" or "The S&P fell 2%." This is the news you can use over time to develop a picture about the direction of the stock market and whether investors are experiencing smooth sailing or choppy waters.

It's also worth noting that with the S&P 500, drastic increases or decreases in a stock's value won't throw off the entire index. Unlike other large-cap indexes like the Dow Jones Industrial Average, the S&P 500 is *market-weighted*, so that no one company or handful of companies experiencing go-go growth will dominate the index or skew its calculations. Market weighting is determined

**market-weighted**
a type of index in which each stock in the index is weighted by its number of outstanding shares, thereby preventing skewed performance.

by multiplying the stock price by the number of *outstanding shares* a company has issued. As a result, no one company's performance distorts the overall performance of the index.

**outstanding shares**
the number of stock shares a company has issued and not bought back.

## The Smart Index

With so many stocks in the computation and with market weighting, the S&P 500 is a broad indicator of market movements. Beat it and you have beaten some of the very finest performers that the U.S. corporate world has to offer. It's also smart, if an index can be considered smart, in the sense that it reflects the wisdom of thousands of analysts and investors who set the market value of the stocks in the index through their own stock purchases and sales.

Outwitting so much brainpower and so successful a portfolio of stocks is a difficult task. Investors, managers included, almost invariably take on far more risk than the index itself has in an attempt to beat the average, and with additional risk they increase the chances that they'll lose ground and take a hit to performance.

What makes the S&P 500 truly so frustrating to money managers is that basic characteristic we talked about earlier in this chapter—it's passive. Its performance reflects what you get in return for doing little more than investing in the stock market as it is defined by a committee at S&P. If so few can beat a passive index, what's the point of hiring a professional manager who charges not insignificant fees for his or her services? Or, for that matter, what's the sense of building your own portfolio and assuming even more risk if you can just invest in a handful of index funds and get performance that's as good or better than most professional managers can produce?

## Autopilot Investing

Those questions are worth asking. With a total of four index funds—a small-cap fund, a large-cap fund, a bond fund, and an international fund—you could with very little time and effort buy the potential rewards and risks

**downside risk**
the risk of losing your principal investment, proportionate to any rewards or performance gains you're likely to get in exchange for those risks.

of all of the securities markets you need to invest for the long term. By using index funds you'd also save yourself money, since they are notoriously less expensive. And you'd cut down on *downside risk*, which you would get if you instead selected securities yourself or paid a regular mutual fund manager, whose one driving force is to beat the index, to try and pick winners for you. As you already know, the odds of him or her doing that are very small.

Ironically, the S&P is a benchmark which by its nature stacks the odds against mutual fund managers. It has no overhead. There's no manager or research department to subsidize. There are no marketing costs or transaction fees, no commissions to salespeople. The average actively managed stock fund has annual expenses of about 1.5%. That means for every $100 you invest, $1.50 of your money goes to pay for the fund's expenses. Right out of the box, because those expenses must be deducted from a mutual fund's or money manager's performance, a manager has huge hurdles to overcome just to match the S&P 500's record.

It's not surprising then that the most popular index for mutual funds to use is—you guessed it—the S&P 500. Index funds can cost as little as 0.2% to manage, according to Gus Sauter, managing director of Vanguard's index funds. There is mounting evidence that low-cost funds beat flashy (or flash-in-the-pan) performers over a time horizon of five or more years. Put another way, if you've got the time, you might want to save the dime—and earn a few extra dimes in the process. With expenses it's important to remember that what is not eaten up in costs is yours to keep, just like it is with your own household budget.

But predictability and low costs aren't the only reasons that S&P 500 index funds have been regular magnets for investor money over the past decade. For much of the 1990s, the S&P 500 has had pure luck on its side. Large-cap stocks have been driving the longest-running bull market in history forward fast. And since it is large-cap stocks that comprise the S&P 500, it's been the hands-down winner of the past five years. In a search of

Standard & Poor's mutual fund data, only 14 diversified equity funds beat the index's annual return of 22.98% for the five years ending with November 1998. (In the five years through November 1998, the S&P 500 returned a cumulative total of 181.3%, including reinvested dividends. This translates into an average annual return of 22.98%.) If you had put money in the S&P 500 three years earlier, it would have doubled as of the end of November 1998. With such daunting performance, it is no wonder index funds have become so popular with investors.

## THE REST OF THE INDEXES

Reverence for the S&P 500 doesn't mean you can or should ignore the other indexes. They are useful when you want to measure the performance of the portion of your assets that they represent, say your small-cap or bond mutual funds, and to determine if your holdings are doing well or poorly relative to their peers. There is an index to measure just about every group of investments.

But what it is important to know about the rest of the indexes is not only how they differ from the S&P 500, but how they differ from one another, even when they seem or purport to be measuring the same piece of investment turf.

**Dow Jones Industrial Average** a well-known index made up of 30 large-cap stocks, which tends to be a psychological indicator, rather than a true measure of the stock market's performance as a whole.

They can also be of assistance when determining how one market, say international stocks, is doing when compared to another, say large-cap stocks. Such comparisons can give you a big-picture understanding of what is going on in the overall markets—which sectors are soaring and which are waning. Here, then, is a look at other pertinent indexes.

### Dow Jones Industrial Average

As well known as it is, the *Dow Jones Industrial Average* tends to be more of a psychological indicator of how the economy is doing than a true measure of the overall stock market's success. It was the brainchild of Charles Dow, who compiled the first industrial average more than a century ago using 12 stocks he believed represented the economy of the late 1890s. Among the first listings were American Cotton Oil, Tennessee Coal, and General Electric—the last of which is the only original stock still on the index. In time, more companies were listed until the current number of 30 stocks was reached, presumably representing the economy as a whole. Current listings include Hewlett-Packard, Johnson & Johnson, and Travelers and are chosen by editors at another one of Dow's creations, the *Wall Street Journal*. While most companies are listed on the New York Stock Exchange, they can be listed on any exchange.

But while most of the Dow's companies are huge, critics argue that there aren't enough of them to represent a true slice of American capitalism at its best, and that's one of the concerns. It is too difficult to imagine that just 30 companies can really represent the vast and diverse U.S. economy. What about industry giants such as Intel or Microsoft, which are conspicuously absent from the Dow? In the latter part of the 1990s, it started to become apparent that the Dow's lack of exposure to high tech—arguably the fastest-growing sector of the U.S. economy in the late 1990s—was causing it to noticeably lag the performance of competing indexes. In 1998, for example, the Dow rose 16.1%, compared to the S&P 500's 26.7% and Nasdaq's 39.6%.

Supporters of the Dow argue that it was never intended to be a hot stock index and will come back into favor if tech stocks fade.

Beyond the limited number of companies on the index, however, there's another shortcoming to contend with. It's a simple fact that the Dow is *price-weighted*—it overweights higher-priced stocks. Since the index focuses on measuring the movement of stock prices without regard to company size or outstanding shares, a smaller company with a high share price will have more impact on the average than a large company with a lower-priced stock. Recently that was the case with AT&T and Caterpillar. AT&T had a lower share price but is three times the size of Caterpillar, yet Caterpillar's

**price-weighted**
a type of index in which stocks are not weighted by a company's size or number of outstanding shares. Unlike a market-weighted index, it over-weights higher-priced stocks.

**unit investment trust**
a collection of stocks which, unlike a mutual fund, is listed on a stock exchange where you can buy and sell shares in it. The portfolio is mostly fixed.

good stock performance actually pulled the overall Dow upward significantly.

That doesn't mean, however, that people don't use the Dow to create mutual funds or other investments. There are three Dow mutual funds with about $140 million in assets, including one run by Waterhouse Securities (compared with 93 S&P index funds with more than $170 billion in assets) that are available to investors.

Dow has also created DIAMONDS, a *unit investment trust* that trades on the American Stock Exchange. You can buy shares or units of the trust, which holds—that's right—the 30 stocks on the Dow. Not surprisingly, it's expected to track the performance of the Dow. The trust differs from a mutual fund mainly because its price can change throughout the trading day and it can be bought and sold on the AMEX, unlike mutual fund shares, which are bought from and sold back to the fund company that created them.

## Nasdaq Composite Index

This rival to the S&P 500 was meant to measure the entire stock market when it was created in the 1970s, but with nearly half its index in telecommunications firms and other high-tech companies, the Nasdaq tends to be significantly more volatile than the stock market at large. It's also, however, the market where some of the most stunning success stories in stock market history have chosen to list their stocks. Microsoft. Yahoo! Amazon.com. Watch a stream of initial public offerings jump from an offering price of $25 or so to an *aftermarket price* of $300 in mere weeks or months, and you'll get the attention of everyone who dreams of wealth.

With high-tech stocks driving the economy overall, and the *Nasdaq Composite Index* listing most of them, it's not surprising that the index has captured the imagination and investment dollars of so many investors and money managers.

In many ways Nasdaq is "The Stock Market of the Next Generation," as its advertisements in the 1990s proclaimed. It was the world's first electronic stock mar-

**aftermarket price**
stock price created after the trading of shares in a company by the original buyers at an initial public offering. This price can be higher or lower than the IPO price.

**Nasdaq Composite Index**
the index that measures the market value of all common stock listed on the Nasdaq Stock Market; highly concentrated in high-tech companies.

ket and it has attracted the likes of Apple, Intel, MCI Communications, Cisco, Oracle, Sun Microsystems, and Netscape. The Nasdaq Composite Index includes the securities of 5,500 companies and is market-weighted, so that larger companies or those with more expensive stock don't skew the overall index. To arrive at its composite figure, it measures the market value of all the domestic and foreign common stocks listed on the Nasdaq Stock Market. Price changes in each security create either a rise or a fall in the index, but only in proportion to their market value. The *market value*—the last-sale price multiplied by total shares outstanding—is calculated continually throughout the trading day. The index was originally set at 100 back in 1971, but has obviously soared, clicking along at about 2,500 as we went to press.

 **market value**
the last sale price multiplied by total shares outstanding of a company's stock.

As the Internet and the companies that were navigating its universe and servicing its users grabbed headlines, certain success stories stood out, even among Nasdaq tales. Take for instance eBay, the online auction company that allows sellers to auction everything from old jazz records and Mercedes-Benzes to new Barbie dolls and Beanie Babies. The stock hit the market at around $30 in the autumn of 1998, rode the market up to a high of $298 on January 28, 1999, then fell $15 the following day and another $62 by February 10, 1999. That would have been merely disappointing news if you had bought at $40 or even $100, but spine-chilling if you had bought at the market high of $298.

Tech stocks aren't alone in driving Nasdaq's volatility. The index is actually made up of eight industry-specific subindexes: banks, biotechnology, computers, finance, industrials, insurance, telecommunications, and transportation.

While it will be increasingly important for investors to watch the Nasdaq Composite and what some of its stocks do, it remains imperative to look at Nasdaq in relation to the S&P 500 and even the Dow to get a sense overall of how the stock market is doing. There are also other slices of the stock market captured by indexes.

## Russell 2000

The *Russell 2000 index* is the most widely used benchmark for small-cap growth stocks, which historically have ruled the market. Created in the mid-1980s, this index tracks 2,000 stocks with an average market share of $250 million. Small caps led the market in the early 1990s, but then hit a slump. Over the past five years, the small-cap Russell 2000 index has risen by 10.3% annually, which seems fine until it's compared with the S&P's more than 20% average annual returns in the same period. The year 1998 was no better for the Russell. It was down 3.34%, while the S&P 500 jumped almost 27%. But that doesn't mean a thing over the long haul: From 1926 through 1997, small U.S. stocks averaged an annual return of 12.7%, versus 11% for large stocks, according to Ibbotson Associates.

**Russell 2000 index**
the most widely used index for gauging the average performance of small-cap growth stocks; includes 2,000 stocks.

## S&P 400, 600, and Global Indexes

**S&P MidCap 400.** The *S&P MidCap 400* index is an attempt by Standard & Poor's to measure mid-cap companies, which are considered to have market capitalizations of under $5 billion. Mid-cap stocks are thought to have almost as much upside potential as small caps, but with less risk.

**S&P MidCap 400**
an index measuring performance of 400 mid-cap stocks.

**S&P SmallCap 600.** This index includes 600 small-cap stocks with market capitalizations under $1 billion. Over $7 billion is indexed to the *S&P SmallCap 600*.

**S&P Global Index.** The *S&P Global Index* includes stocks listed on the Toronto Stock Exchange as well as companies from the United Kingdom, Latin America, Japan, and the Asia/Pacific region.

**S&P SmallCap 600**
an index measuring performance of 600 small-cap stocks.

## Wilshire Indexes

**Wilshire 5000.** This index tracks nearly all of the stocks listed on the NYSE, the AMEX, and the Nasdaq Stock Market, so it gives investors an overall picture of how the large, mid-, and small-cap markets are doing. Its name, however, is something of a misnomer because it

**S&P Global Index**
an index that includes international stocks.

tracks the performance of almost every publicly traded stock, far more than 5,000 stocks. It has a following as well as a group of index funds that track its performance, including the company's own Wilshire 5000 Index Portfolio. New in 1999, the fund owns about 2,000 stocks, including the largest stocks.

**Wilshire 4500.** This index is the Wilshire 5000 minus the S&P 500. This index picks up the smaller-cap stocks that constitute the rest of the market. Vanguard Index Extended Market uses the Wilshire 4500 as its benchmark.

**Wilshire Small Company Growth.** This index includes fast-growing small-cap companies.

**Wilshire Small Company Value.** This index looks at small companies that are undervalued compared to their faster-growing peers.

### Morgan Stanley Indexes

**Morgan Stanley Capital International Emerging Markets Index.** This index includes smaller companies operating in up-and-coming and also sometimes highly volatile developing markets around the world.

**Morgan Stanley Capital International Europe, Australia, Asia, and Far East (EAFE) Index.** This index tracks more than one thousand foreign stocks in 20 different countries. It is considered one of the more prominent international indexes. Both Vanguard International Index Europe and Vanguard International Index Pacific invest in the respective regional stocks in this index.

### Lehman Brothers Indexes

**Lehman Brothers Aggregate Bond Index.** As the name suggests, this index represents a collection of bonds including Treasuries, corporate bonds, mortgage-backed bonds, and asset-backed bonds. The Vanguard Bond Index mirrors this index.

**Lehman Brothers Long-Term High Quality Government/Corporate Bond Index.** This broad-based index tracks the performance of the universe of high-quality government and corporate bonds that have maturities of 15 to 30 years. High quality means that most of the bonds are rated A or better by Moody's Investors Service.

## A WORD TO THE WISE

While some people believe that beating the indexes is the be-all and end-all of investing, the fact is that a handful of stocks or even bonds in any of the indexes we've cited here can really make or break the overall index's performance. In other words, if you didn't happen to own one or more of those particular stocks or bonds, or a mutual fund that invested in those stocks or bonds, you're unlikely to beat the index's performance.

But you don't have to take our word for it. Salomon Smith Barney, the mammoth New York City–based brokerage house, found that in 1998, 75% of the stocks in the S&P 500 actually lagged the index's performance by a whopping 15%. In fact, one might argue that the top 24 stocks in the index, led by Amazon.com (which gave investors a 966% return in 1998), America Online (a 585.6% return), and Yahoo! (a 584% return), were almost solely responsible for the S&P's sizzle that year.

Of course, everything is relative. Most investors throughout history (with the exception of those who think they can beat the odds in Las Vegas) would have been perfectly satisfied with the S&P's return—a robust 28%. But many investors weren't. Not when 500%-plus returns were touted repeatedly on the evening news and in banner headlines.

"That's what's driving investors into stocks," says Jim Bruyette, a partner in the financial planning firm of Sullivan, Bruyette, Speros & Blayney, in McLean, Virginia. "The difference between these stocks and more diversified investment strategies is so extreme." But the best approach, he adds, is not to engage in short-term trading strategies such as day trading, but to buy good companies and hold them.

One more fact to consider: Many people brag about their investment returns. Many others claim it is their right and duty to beat—not meet, mind you, but beat—the S&P. Well, anyone who achieved an overall 28% return in 1998 should have been very happy indeed, since the majority of investors earned less than 10% on their overall investment portfolios.

# All the Business
# News That Fits

Technology, shmechnology. If you're someone who likes to hold a good ol' American newspaper between your fingers over coffee, not to worry. Despite the rise of TV business news and the never-ending stream of Internet investment information, there is still plenty of important and timely information to be gleaned in the old-fashioned way—from the business press. In fact, you can find significantly more information now than you could even a decade ago, when more than half of the big personal finance magazines didn't even exist and only a handful of daily newspapers had reporters who even knew what a mutual fund was.

From specialized newspapers such as *Barron's*, *Investor's Business Daily*, and the *Wall Street Journal*, to the national general-interest newspapers with big business sections such as the *New York Times* and *USA Today*, to magazines like *Business Week*, the *Economist*, and *SmartMoney*, there is more investing and personal finance information than any one person—short of a money manager with staff—can use.

## WHAT TO LOOK FOR

The good news is you don't need to read all of these publications to be informed. Anyone who does read them all or even many of them quickly realizes how much redundancy and repetition there is. You don't have to read the same story four different times to be informed. Still, the publications are not all the same. You should know which best serves your information needs and investment strategy. You really can benefit from knowing how to take advantage of the best features of each.

Christopher Woodbridge in Washington, DC, an investor who bought his first mutual fund just two years ago and now also invests in his 401(k) plan at United Parcel Service, likes *Investor's Business Daily* for its technology news and the *Wall Street Journal* for what he calls "the big picture stuff."

Woodbridge says, "I've gotten to the point now where I can skim the papers, looking for what interests me, in about 20 to 30 minutes a day. I look for new investments, but I also check out the ones I have and look for related stories. I think of it as part of my investment activities, actually. It's the only way I know of monitoring my progress."

What should you be looking for? Here's a primer on the type of news that investors zero in on and the type of stories that will give you an understanding of which investments are winning in the investment markets, which are on their way up, and which are on their way down.

### *Our Markets*

What is going on with the S&P 500? The Dow Jones Industrial Average? The Nasdaq Stock Market? How are large company stocks performing? What about mid and small company stocks? Are 30-year Treasury yields climbing or receding? Depending on what you own and what you're interested in, these types of stories can be important to understanding how you're doing in relation to the pertinent markets you're invested in. News about different investments is also important. For instance, if investors are suddenly pouring money into stock mutual funds or pulling their money out (called redemptions), it is an indication of investor confidence or lack of it.

## Think Globally

While the United States has felt like the only game in town—and even in the world—for several years now, investing really is global. With bureaus overseas, the *Wall Street Journal* routinely reports on trends in small and large company performance in countless countries, on the major economies of the world, and on their stock markets and social and political environments.

## Company Profiles

Part of your research is to "kick the tires," as analysts and professional investors call this qualitative analysis. That means knowing what the company makes or what services it sells. Decent stories should tell you how the market for pertinent products and services is faring, how well the company is faring in those markets, how well management performs, whether there are strengths and weaknesses, and how the company is perceived by its competitors and customers.

## Behind the Dollars

Understanding the role the Federal Reserve Board plays in setting policy and influencing markets is important even for individual investors. Your portfolio, and the stock and bond markets, will rise and fall as a result of the Fed's actions. Being able to distinguish short-term responses from more fundamental shifts—that is, separating reactions to Fed chairman Alan Greenspan's public statements from effects of the Fed's move to raise or lower some interest rates—will make you less susceptible to panic moves.

Greenspan can move markets with his comments, but the markets tend to recover quickly from his cautions. (His notable assessment of the stock market as being propelled by "irrational exuberance" that had led to its being dramatically overpriced was widely repeated for years after he made the statement. It is worthwhile noting that these were also years when the market continued to climb.)

The Fed raising interest rates can slow the economy and as a result lower stock market growth, which in turn can lower your return. That's a longer-term factor and you may want to adjust your portfolio accordingly—shifting, say, to value-oriented investments over growth investments.

### Savvy Investing

Part of the reason you read is to become a better, more confident investor. The more you read, the more you develop your perspective on investments and how they work and respond to news and events. This will give you depth as an investor. You'll be far less likely to buy or sell without doing the appropriate research. And you'll develop your own investment philosophy. People who stick with an investment philosophy or discipline tend to be more successful than those who hop around trying to get in on investment successes after the fact. It's fine to use a portion of your portfolio to invest in some of the hotter sectors or stocks, but put the majority of your money in long-term investments you plan to hold for years.

## THE BUSINESS PRESS

In Chapter 9 we'll help you select a short list of magazines to include in your periodical library. For now, let's take a close-up look at the best of what the business press—our nation's newspapers—has to offer.

## The Wall Street Journal

It's easy for new investors to feel daunted by the great grayness of the Wall Street Journal. With more than 1.7 million subscribers, the premier financial newspaper in the world has a large following and it is attempting to meet the needs of just about all of them. Traditional business news in the Journal is predictably thorough. Its news stories appear scrupulously balanced, in contrast to its archly conservative editorial pages.

The paper is divided into three daily sections, each providing distinct coverage. They are: the "A" or news section, the "B" or "Marketplace" section, and the "C" or "Money & Investing" section. The first section contains breaking news and features on companies, the economy, legal news, and trends both in the United States and abroad. The "Marketplace" section focuses on business profiles and trends and includes columns on technology, health, advertising, and other subjects. The "Money & Investing" section offers the hard data and analysis that was once the dominant content of the newspaper.

Professional investors, money managers, traders, and investment bankers see the Journal as required reading, though you don't have to read it all. You can pick and choose what you need from its offerings, which are as broad and deep as you'll find probably anywhere. If you don't own or aren't interested in bonds, or personal computer stocks, or a particular mutual fund, by all means zero in on what does interest you. The important thing is not to overwhelm yourself, because too much of a good thing really is bad.

What you can expect is some fine reporting and writing that is likely to engage you in behind-the-scenes views of business leaders, politicians, and the man and woman on the street. Although the stories are most often about business, management, politics, and economics, the Journal is willing to devote considerable space in the first and second sections to offbeat topics (for instance, the comeback of male hair "comb-overs" and the trials of using synthetic shoelaces are two recent stories that come to mind). While these stories have delicious entertainment value, they are also educational. Since *Journal* reporters are often a step ahead of their competition when it comes to spotting and exploiting trends, you may want to ask yourself what any interesting story may mean to societal tastes and mores—in other words, where Americans and even world investors are putting their investment dollars. See if you can spot any trends that come to fruition in the near term. These stories can also give you insight into companies and their founders, executives, and managers that analyst reports and less in-depth reporting can't touch.

So the pithy journalism shouldn't be ignored, even if it is the great gray data and the articles on company and market performance found mostly in the Money & Investing section that investors typically seek first from the *Journal*. Regulatory investigations are headlined here; so are accounting snafus, fraud, news about the latest brokerage scandal, and the trends impacting every major investment. If a company lied to shareholders in its annual report, or a band of bad brokers is trying to pawn off fraudulent investments onto unsuspecting investors, you'll read it here. This is also the place to turn to look for how individual investments and the markets overall are performing.

The *WSJ*'s Money & Investing section is also a good place to learn about how various approaches to market analysis—quantitative, technical, growth versus value, and so on—are applied by economists and money managers in real-time, real-world settings.

To best understand this key section of the newspaper, think of it as organized into several topics or subject areas. The market news of the day in the "Abreast of the Market" column is often a leading item, particularly when stock and bond markets are soaring or declining. Writers talk to a variety of money professionals to get their interpretations about where the markets are headed. This is a very good place to learn about market volatility. You'll get clear, concise accounts of what is going on in the economy or a particular market, which will give you a good idea of how much you can gain and lose when you invest.

"Heard on the Street" is another column that can move markets, that is, literally move stock prices up and down on the basis of what is said in the column. It generally focuses on a sector of the market, like banking or technology, and analyzes the pertinent trends shaping the industry. Put those two columns at the top of your priority list. "Your Money Matters" and "Inside Track" are two other columns you should read. You'll quickly discover the column headings are in many cases interchangeable. The point is to give yourself a sense of what the market and individual stocks are doing.

Don't forget to check out the "Markets Diary" on page C1, which gives you last night's close for the Dow Jones Industrial Average and other U.S. stock indexes; international stock indexes, including those based on stock exchanges in London, Paris, and Tokyo; and bonds indexes for corporate bonds, long Treasury bonds, mortgage bonds, and municipal bonds. And, of course, check the benchmarks of market performance in this section. Results for most indexes and benchmarks are listed for the day, year-to-date, and preceding 12 months. This is also where you'll generally find a complete table of bond market data.

Money & Investing also includes columns on world markets, *futures*, *options*, and all types of mutual funds from growth-oriented large U.S. stock mutual funds to hybrid funds like oil and energy. The section also critiques more insurance-oriented investments such as annuities (which act as a tax-deferred wrapper for mutual fund investors to buy for retirement) and a dozen other investment vehicles. Follow those that interest you first, and later you'll be able to choose the ones that match your portfolio and your investment strategy.

After reading the market analyses, look at the stock, bond, and mutual fund listings. This is where you go to track those investments you're interested in as well as those that are in your portfolio's performance—or if you prefer, you can do this online.

**futures**
contracts to buy or sell a set number of shares of a specific stock or a set amount of some commodity at a future date and price. The contracts themselves are traded on futures markets.

**options**
the rights to either buy or sell a set number of shares of a stock at a specified price within a specified amount of time—even if the market price of that stock is less or more than the price specified by the option. An option differs from a future in that you are not required to use the option to sell or buy.

Overloaded yet? Data creep is a huge issue among some financial analysts and journalists who worry that there are some investors who believe that gathering just one more fact will somehow make everything—investing, the must-have mutual fund, to-die-for stocks—crystal clear. That is an easy trap to slip into. While technical analysts may love to gather facts, the rest of us investors can get overwhelmed and end up overthinking our choices.

One way to assess this onslaught of information as you start investing is to recall the basic measures of performance outlined in Chapter 6, so you're not distracted by what might actually be miscellaneous, if noteworthy, fluff about a company. These performance measures include total return and price-earnings ratio, earnings per share, cash flow, and dividends paid for stocks. It's a good idea to rely at least in part on these basic measures to make decisions.

More technically oriented? Then by nature you'll seek out additional information, say on the direction of individual markets over the course of the month or year. You can find this kind of information under "Stock Market Data Bank" or "NYSE Highs/Lows" and in various charts (e.g., "Money Flow") that are scattered throughout the section.

With those tasks completed, you can move to the other two sections of the *Journal*. Your first aim is to identify any stories about stocks, bonds, and mutual funds you already own. Keeping track of Microsoft, or the Magellan Fund, or the success your state had selling bonds is an important part of monitoring your portfolio. Reading that the manager of an underperforming fund you hold has been replaced can either encourage you to stay invested or be the last straw.

Next, be on the lookout for new investing opportunities, which you can glean from profiles on companies that might fit your strategy. Look for merger news as well. Wall Street almost always rewards the target of a merger with a higher price and penalizes the company doing the buying. If you own the target, you'll know to hang on for the bounce. If you own the buyer, you won't be surprised when share price drops.

Be sure to check the editorial pages, too. There you'll find one of the more curious anomalies in print journalism. On the left you'll read fairly right-wing interpretations of current events, which are produced by the *Journal's* editorial writers. On the right page, you'll often find the writings and interpretations of the *Journal's* senior editors, including Washington bureau chief Al Hunt, who have a more liberal bent. This is truly a page at war with itself, though the battle often serves to supply investors with the full array of arguments available on any given topic.

**WSJ Online (www.wsj.com).** The *Wall Street Journal's* news site attempts to look like the print version of the *Wall Street Journal*, but there is more to it than that, including hot-off-the-press Dow Jones news stories. The online archive contains articles from both sources from the past 14 days. Its searches can yield stories on almost any financial subject. It is perhaps the most impressive article search feature available for investors. Some of the Dow Jones features run exclusively on the web site, so you won't know about them unless you have looked there.

### Barron's

Dow Jones publishes both the *Wall Street Journal* and something of a sister publication, *Barron's. Barron's* is a financial and business weekly. Aside from the musings of one of its lead columnists, Alan Abelson, which are sometimes more stylistic than analytic, *Barron's* is jargon-free and explanatory without being overly simplistic. Most *Barron's* writers assume that an explanation of terms and concepts is as much a requirement of the story as actual news. That's no mean feat to pull off without insulting readers, but the tabloid does a fine job, especially when you consider that the stories are written for fairly sophisticated readers.

One piece on predicting market movement deftly outlined the dismal history of economists' attempts to declare when bull or bear markets start. The story explained that few economists recognize the beginning of a bear market in time to do anything about it—like sell investments before the market crashes. It also outlined the history of seven recent bear markets and of the four recessions that were linked to these market downturns. The story included enough facts to prove the tabloid's arguments. For investors seeking information and insight, the story included useful advice that outlined which economic signs might signal a Federal Reserve move to stave off the next recession.

*Barron's* isn't the *Wall Street Journal*. It does not have the wide-spanning news coverage. It's a weekly, of course, which means that it is more focused because it has less space to deal with the economy, markets, investments, companies, and players. It accomplishes its work mostly with eight or so feature stories and a dozen regular columns covering the stock and bond markets, breaking news, and, yes, the economy.

Whether you're hankering to invest online or are already an old hand, the "Electronic Investor" column is a good source of new sites written with the clear eye of someone who knows how to select some of the must-have articles without overwhelming readers. Too often, Internet site analysis ends up telling you to bookmark nearly every site for some reason or other. That is overload. The "Electronic Investor" column manages to winnow the list to just a few discriminating choices.

The *Barron's* stories and columns are wrapped around "Market Week," a bulky report on the markets that includes regular columnists and data on the markets, leading indicators of market performance, indexes, and weekly performance of stocks, bonds, and mutual funds. The amount of information in this section and in the charts is enormous. Under stocks, for instance, *Barron's* lists *ticker symbol*, 52-week high and low price information, P/Es, actual and estimated earnings, and dividends. This helpful chart is an oversized box that

**ticker symbol**
the abbreviation used to represent a company's stock in its listing on the appropriate stock exchange.

runs each week. The explanation is a minidictionary of investment terms.

Generally, if you're an investor getting started, you'd pick either the *Wall Street Journal* or *Barron's* to read, depending on your preferences, but not necessarily both.

***Barron's* Online (www.barrons.com).** This is a good site for finding out what mutual fund managers think and what investors think. The site just started an "Ask the Manager" section, which allows you to ask the managers of those funds you invest in—or are interested in investing in—what they're doing in response to market changes and why they're investing in particular stocks, bonds, or cash.

## *Investor's Business Daily*

This California-based newspaper is a tech investor's dream, filled with data on thousands of stocks and mutual funds. The newspaper, founded by market strategist and broker William J. O'Neil in 1984, is an extension of O'Neil's own highly developed computer investment models, which are aimed at predicting stock price movement.

*Investor's Business Daily*, by design, limits its coverage of breaking news to only the biggest stories, using its "National Issue" lead position on page one mostly for interpretive articles on a relatively narrow range of topics. In recent years, the newspaper has gone to great lengths to beef up its mutual fund and personal finance coverage under the leadership of editors such as Doug Rogers, who is seen by money managers as one of the best and brightest critics of the fund industry.

The broadsheet newspaper also provides scores of company profiles under its "New America" and "Computers & Technology" page headings. Use these profiles as starting points for building a portfolio. Be aware, however, that these stories almost invariably feature smaller- and mid-cap companies, often high-tech concerns, and always high-earnings-growth firms. As for technology, however, *IBD* really does walk the talk—it even has a news bureau in Silicon Valley. These companies are usually riskier investments than big blue-chip stocks. The mutual funds profiled, however, tend to fall into the growth and blue-chip categories, where risk is lower.

The newspaper makes extensive use of letter and percentile grading systems. Its market commentary is comprehensive, though generally aimed at more savvy readers, especially those familiar with O'Neil's investing concepts, which generally involve a good deal more buying and selling than the average investor will probably feel comfortable with—at least initially. Various tables and data detailing different investments' performance and measuring different kinds of market activity are clearly written. One that O'Neil himself says he uses first when he gets his paper is the "Where the Big Money's Flowing" chart, which appears at the beginning of the stock tables. The chart shows the increase in trading volume in both NYSE- and Nasdaq-traded stocks above their average trading volume, which may demonstrate what mutual funds, pensions, and institutional money managers are buying and selling.

"The Big Picture" column on *Investor Business Daily*'s General Market page provides readers with a professional summary of the important happenings in the market with a step-by-step, numbered analysis pointing to key indicators on the accompanying charts.

That's a good deal of information, but there really isn't any mystery to this paper, because of the step-by-step instructions and cross references contained throughout. That's one of the nice things about *Investor's Business Daily*—many of the stories also contain explanations on how to use the rest of the newspaper to compare investments and see which are doing well and which are floundering.

The "Making Money in Mutuals" section offers more interviews with mutual fund managers than most other publications. Its "Basics" column provides instruction for beginning investors. The "Investment Trends" column and "Meet the Manager" profiles offer insight on a variety

of topics and on successful investing strategies professional money managers use. This helps you get a feel for
how those who are paid to follow and buy stocks select
from the ocean that is available.

The charts include typical performance data on mutual funds as well as an *IBD*-generated performance grade
from A+ on down to D, based on the fund's total return for
the preceding 36 months. The charts also include portfolio content, turnover rate, and the various risk measures
that are applied to mutual funds.

Touting itself as an alternative to the *Wall Street Journal*, not just a competitor, *IBD* also offers personal finance
and personal improvement advice and profiles of successful individuals under its "Leaders and Success" banner.
The editorial page offers a spirited defense of the free market system and individual enterprise.

**Reading the Charts.** The charts are more comprehensive than you find in most other financial publications,
reflecting O'Neil's technical approach to investing. He
tells investors it can take two years or more to master the
data contained in *IBD*. This may well be true. To speed
that process are explanatory tables that appear regularly
in the newspaper. You can find further help for interpret-
ing the information in O'Neil's *How to Make Money in
Stocks* (McGraw-Hill, 1995), which explains his methodology. Few publications pay as much attention to aiding
readers in using their products as does *IBD*.

**IBD Online (www.investors.com).** *IBD*'s news site is
among the leanest of the major financial newspapers' sites.
It doesn't offer breaking news headlines or stock quotes,
and it won't keep tabs on your portfolio for you. But as a
source of business leaders profiles, company and market
analysis, and basic but precise information about the markets and mutual funds, it is probably the easiest and fastest
to use of the major financial publications' sites. As helpful,
*IBD*'s archives run back to the mid-1990s. There is also an
index at the web site that depicts the current issue's content, including the newspaper's "National Issue" story of
the day and its "Top 10" stories of the day list.

# NATIONAL NEWSPAPERS

### The New York Times

Heavy on economic analysis and market performance, the *Times* business section also provides plenty of company profiles and thorough coverage of breaking news like management changes, corporate performance, and earnings surprises. Its mutual fund coverage is concentrated in its Sunday edition. The mutual fund manager profiles, the only real portion of mutual fund analysis that can't be shown in a table or graph, are usually comprehensive, or at least lengthy. For anyone with a professional interest in mutual funds, the stories are useful. For investors, especially those who are not investors in a specific fund, the news may be overly specific.

But if you are an investor in a specific fund, say the Baron Fund, reading about your colorful and outspoken leader, Ron Baron, is not only entertaining but also informative. Unlike many fund managers, Baron all but moves in with the management of the companies he has in his fund. He'll tell you his version of events at the drop of a hat. It's insight you won't find elsewhere. When you get this acquainted with your mutual fund managers, you might even be able to predict what they'll do during different markets.

**NYT Online (www.nytimes.com).** This is almost like nicking a copy of the *Times* from a newsstand. You can breeze into the web site, read the current online issue, and move on. Keep in mind, however, that you miss much of the data and benchmark information contained in the newspaper.

### USA Today

Consistently the sweetened and condensed version of the news, *USA Today* is nonetheless a useful source of financial information, especially breaking stories. This is where its brevity is no longer a shortcoming because the paper seems to know how to consistently pack a great deal of relevant information into a tight space.

Its company profiles are examples of the best kind of brevity. A feature on Lands' End's problems in the crowded catalog marketplace is analytical, outlining sales and profits statistics at the big clothing catalog firm, while addressing both Lands' End's specific problems and the mail order industry's woes—all in under 1,100 words.

As for reading the charts, there is nothing here that's groundbreaking, though it is easy to understand *USA Today*'s charts and tables. But that's the point of the paper.

*USA Today* **Online (www.usatoday.com).** It's no surprise that this web site is colorful. It's busy looking, but packed with links to useful information like Lipper Analytical Services and Zacks Investment Research. The former is a good source of performance information on various kinds of mutual funds—growth and income, for instance, or small-cap. The latter is the place to look for performance information on stocks, analysts' recommendations, and so forth. *USA Today*'s news site is also a reliable source to find out about promising new investment-related web sites. Search its own site for stories about stocks and mutual funds you're considering.

There is also a link to online calculators and Banxquote, which is a guide to the best interest rates in your state.

One feature of the news site's "Money" section that is useful to investors is a list of links to various subsections of the money page, like mutual funds and banking, Wall Street summary, and initial public offerings. When web sites condense the search options this way, you can move quickly to the information you need.

The broader search feature reveals the weakness of search engines in general. It delivers plenty of citations, but at this writing none of the stories is labeled with a date, so you don't often know if you are reading a story from last week or last year or even earlier. For an investor, that's a fairly serious shortcoming. Nothing is as meaningless or misleading to an unknowing investor as a story about the stock market in 1997. So unless there's a date on it—read with caution.

## Washington Post

**Washington Post Online (www.washingtonpost. com).** If you're wondering what's going on in Washington, in the form of either Federal Reserve Board news, White House initiatives, or Congressional activities, this is the place to go. You'll also find Washington area companies profiled here.

Chapter

# Personal Finance Periodicals

Financial journalists never thought they'd see the day when there were more personal finance magazines than gossipy tabloids hanging off the racks at the supermarket checkout counter, but that day has arrived. You can thank the decade-long bull market of the 1990s for the crowded personal finance advice market.

But more doesn't necessarily mean better. In any given month, writers at four or five different magazines might come up with substantially different takes on the same story. In one magazine, small-cap stocks and small-cap mutual funds may be the dogs of the decade, while in another they're the value buy of the year.

To truly be a devotee of the investment magazines such as *Kiplinger's*, *SmartMoney*, and *Money*, you'd have to buy and sell mutual funds en masse every month when the magazines create new lists of must-have mutual funds. The problem? Many of the funds they pick never make it onto their must-have lists twice. So you'll have to either keep replacing the ones you buy every time one of their new lists comes out or buy so many funds your portfolio becomes unwieldy, impossible to monitor, and probably redundant—meaning that you probably own identical stocks and bonds in numerous mutual funds. Trading mutual funds or stocks may make someone sound like a Wall Street operator to anyone who doesn't know any better. But, as we've already reported, the actual costs and commissions associated with frequent trading will eat into your profits.

"Personal finance periodicals can be worth reading, but you have to remember that they have an inherent conflict of interest," says Christopher Parr, principal of Parr Financial Solutions in Columbia, Maryland. "Their job is to generate excitement to sell magazines, so writers tend to chase the flavor of the month. But if you're after a long-term investment strategy, basically you want to be pretty boring," Parr says. In the case of investments, boring is good.

You have to step back and assess the information magazines are selling you based on the facts. Just as you would with investment advice from a neighbor or even an accountant, broker, insurance salesperson, or financial planner, remember to put any advice you read in a personal finance magazine to the test. Is what they're telling you valid or does it just sound good? From your reading, do you know something about the investment they're touting that they haven't mentioned that might make it a good or bad buy? What's your independent read of the investment, say of a mutual fund, if you look at its performance track record? If it's a stock, what's your read of consumer and investor perception, the company's market, management, and financial positioning? Does its P/E make it attractive?

All investments go through periods of outperformance and underperformance. A mutual fund that is touted in the magazines for its recent strong performance may actually be headed for a period when its investment style is out of favor. Conversely, when an investment has been on the outs just long enough that you're ready to sell (and it has become the official whipping boy of magazine writers), it may be headed for a miraculous recovery or turnaround.

No magazine or pile of them is the be-all and end-all of investment advice. "You have to decide what your goals and your risk tolerance are," says Lou Stana- solovich, a financial planner and president of Legend Financial Advisors, Inc., in Pittsburgh, Pennsylvania. "Then find an investment with a substantial enough track record that matches up. No magazine can do that for you," he adds.

Still and all, magazines can be a great source of information. They can bring to your attention some solid mutual funds, stocks, and bonds that you may never have noticed (provided you put the investments through your own checks before investing). They can also give you a spate of very important financial planning advice, like how to make the most of your IRAs (individual retirement accounts), minimize the income taxes you pay, get the best home equity loan, or decide how much life insurance you might need and buy it on the cheap.

Here's our list of the magazines you'll want to sample from at the bookstore or library before deciding which ones work for you.

## MAGAZINES FOR INDIVIDUAL INVESTORS

### *Bloomberg Personal*

A newcomer to an increasingly crowded field, *Bloomberg Personal* is the *Atlantic Monthly* of finance magazines, offering thoughtful, thorough articles often by well-known financial writers. The magazine is a part of the Bloomberg financial information conglomerate that includes a news service, radio show, and television program. Surprisingly, however, the magazine draws on few of the technical resources available to it, relying instead on its writers' insights.

The magazine intentionally skews its coverage to those who have higher net worth and a good bit of investment sophistication. The assumption seems to be that it is drawing its audience from the same demographic group as those who subscribe to its other services.

Still, *Bloomberg's* range of story topics is similar to the other personal finance magazines and includes company profiles, market commentary, trends, and the usual roundup of stories on retirement planning, investing in your home, teaching your kids about cash, and where to spend your money for a good time—vacations, collecting, and the like.

What's different is the presence of heavy hitter economists like Nancy Kimelman, chief economist of Technical Data, and analysts such as David Shulman, the chief equity strategist at Salomon Brothers; Joseph V. Battipaglia, chief investment strategist at Gruntal & Company; and Charles Hill, director of research at First Call Corporation, a firm that offers real-time equity research online (www.firstcall.com).

To be sure, *Bloomberg* allows certain Wall Street experts to have their say. But the magazine's careful editing and its well-developed sense of its role to the reader mean the columns and essays aren't simply self-promotion.

Founder Michael Bloomberg makes no apologies for the highbrow reader he seeks. In his welcoming letter to subscribers, he describes the magazine as aimed solely at sophisticated, upper-income investors. Still, there are articles that can be helpful to all investors, such as ones about diversification, finding funds that trade infrequently, and mastering your money emotions to maximize your investment returns.

***Bloomberg* Online (www.bloomberg.com).** This site is not a strong entry, which is surprising from a company built on high-tech computer terminals. Still, you get access to Bloomberg News, which can be useful as a research source, particularly if you are investing overseas or in bonds and other fixed income securities, since the news service provides good, breaking coverage of the fixed income markets.

### Individual Investor

Another newcomer, *Individual Investor*, offers the best introduction to investing of the major financial magazines.

The magazine's instructional section, "The Educated Investor," offers readers the liveliest and most readable
primer in personal finance, an area other investment magazines have all but abandoned. Read this first for helpful
tips on getting started, narrowing the field of investments
you might be considering, and hedging your bets, so
you're more at ease. You'll also get a sense from this section of what you can expect when you invest, and what
types of investments you should steer clear of until you
have some solid experience (and a few down markets) under your belt.

With mostly lively writing, the magazine overall
manages to deliver on the promise of its title, with little
of the extraneous information like vacation advice or
personal improvement that sometimes seems to dominate other personal finance publications. Content
ranges from company profiles to basic instruction, insight on the market, profiles of mutual fund managers,
and the performance of the mutual fund and stock portfolios the magazine created. Those portfolios have delivered mixed results, for which the magazine makes no
apologies.

There's also small company information galore. The
magazine's INDI SmallCap 500, a benchmark index it
created, follows a constantly updated list of 500 small
cap companies that engage in an array of businesses including, of course, technology and Internet products
and services.

### *Individual Investor* Online (www.iionline.com).

This site is among the strongest web pages of the personal
finance magazines and very news oriented. The stock and
sector analysis is impressive, dissecting hot stocks, mergers like the one between Broadcast.com and Yahoo!, and
undervalued stocks. Any investors looking for information on where to put money next will find these sections
useful. Only Morningstar offers more mutual fund screening capability to help you find funds that meet your investment goals. America Online's mutual fund search is
slow by comparison. The portfolio tracking page here in-

cludes a column for sales commission, unusual in online portfolio tracking services, and is very useful in determining your exact total return, including the cost of each transaction you make.

*Individual Investor*'s online magazine appears to contain nearly everything in the current issue. That's also unusual among publications struggling with how to make the Internet pay and unwilling, as a result, to give away what they sell on paper. Don't forget to use its premier learning tool for new investors—its "Educated Investor" column.

The Screening Room's "America's Fastest Growing Companies," which *Individual Investor* has trademarked, epitomizes the magazine's ability to merge its own computer databases (the magazine is owned by a *hedge fund*) to effectively screen for high-growth companies. Street Beaters is a list of stocks that have surprised analysts by beating earnings estimates. Hot Stocks is a screen of stocks hitting new share price highs. Insider's Edge is a screen of companies whose management has recently purchased or sold shares. That is often an indication of insider confidence, or the lack of it, in a company. There's also Uncommon Value, where online investors can question *Individual Investor*'s very own analysts.

**hedge fund**
a fund that may use many complex techniques based on valuation models to enhance its return, such as both buying and borrowing shares of a stock.

## *Kiplinger's Personal Finance Magazine*

The first personal finance magazine, now more than 50 years old, *Kiplinger's* is a full-service financial publication offering basic investment instruction, stock and mutual fund picks, and profiles of professional and amateur investors. About half of the magazine is devoted to a comprehensive range of investing topics. Unlike *Individual Investor* or *SmartMoney*, *Kiplinger's* does not routinely create portfolios and then follow their performance in subsequent issues. As a result, you don't really get a sense of how well the magazine's investment picks and strategies work.

The in-depth, question-and-answer "Insider Interviews" with prominent mutual fund managers can be useful, however, even if you're not interested in investing in
the fund. You'll get a sense of top managers' investment
styles, why they steer clear of certain sectors, and what
they think will happen in the next year or so. Covering
every accepted investment strategy from value to growth
investing, the interviews with the likes of Mario Gabelli
get you inside the minds of some noteworthy market gurus. It's interesting to see how sometimes they make decisions with little more than a hunch to go on, while at
other times they're armed to the teeth with charts and analysts' recommendations.

*Kiplinger's* also publishes comprehensive performance rankings for hundreds of mutual funds several
times a year. The data, always comprehensive, rivals most
investment publications for its thoroughness and useful
information, like the toll-free phone numbers of just
about any mutual fund you can think of.

***Kiplinger's* Online (www.kiplinger.com).** This web
site is user-friendly and offers a search option of back issues of the magazine. The search is disappointing, however, because it seems unable to yield the number of
stories you would expect on topics such as first-time investing or risk tolerance. Selected stories from the current
issue are also available online. As an added draw, the web
site features breaking business news from Reuters and a
portfolio tracker. The magazine's television program is
syndicated in about 100 markets and those outlets are
listed on the web page.

## Money

The much reinvented *Money* magazine has finally come
down out of the clouds that afflicted so many financial
magazines in the 1980s. When it came to financial reality, the sky was the limit back then. No extravagance

seemed too expensive or overpriced. Ironically, the early 1990s burst the yuppie bubble, if only a bit, and most financial magazines became refreshingly pragmatic, offering real-life solutions to real-life problems. Then, in the mid-1990s, the stock market took off again and most magazines, *Money* included, began focusing on useful investing information. *Money*, like most of the financial magazines, is more practical today, but it does seem to have lost some of its verve in the process. For real sass, see *SmartMoney.*

Like *Kiplinger's*, *Money* publishes extensive analysis on mutual funds several times a year. It also produces some very interesting stories on the successes and failures of new investors.

**Money Online (www.money.com).** *Money's* web page is a tightly laid out and well-organized guide to money and investing. While it offers much of what you find on any personal finance web site, namely stock quotes and market data, it manages to pique your interest with perhaps two dozen citations of stories from the magazine and links to other web pages.

It isn't flashy, but it is surprisingly user-friendly. We found stories on the best personal finance software, tips on where to find the lowest mortgage rates, and a series on how to plan for each financial stage of your life—from your early twenties through retirement.

The *Money* web page also offers real-time quotes to those who register for the free service. As an added bonus, there are also links to other parts of the Time Inc. magazine empire, including *Fortune*, *Time*, and *People*.

### Mutual Funds Magazine

What makes *Mutual Funds* magazine such an attractive read is its ability to report on the mutual fund industry in a way individual investors can find meaningful. The stories of changes in fund management, which often condense what are clearly bloody battles of succession into cool prose, help investors understand the philosophies and strategies that can make fund managers successful. The more you know about these surrogate financial advisers you've enlisted to make you rich, the better you understand whether you are becoming rich as the years go by.

**_Mutual Funds_ Magazine Online (www.mfmag. com).** This is a helpful site to give investors perspective regarding what sectors of the economy and stock market are hot or about to be hot. The site chooses a stock of the month, which you can follow over time to see how on target the writers' recommendations are. The site also features long-term stock and mutual fund winners; recently included were funds from Alger and Fidelity that have winning 5- and 10-year records.

### SmartMoney

_SmartMoney_ is a collaboration between the Hearst Corporation publishing company and Dow Jones, the publisher of the _Wall Street Journal_ and _Barron's_. _SmartMoney_ hit the stands running with a powerful package of high-profile writers, many from the _Wall Street Journal_, and attractive graphics and design. In a field fraught with boilerplate wisdom that is too routinely repeated, _SmartMoney_ has managed with a series of articles labeled "Ten Things Your Broker Won't Tell You" or the like to offer fresh, useful information.

    _SmartMoney_ is aimed at a knowledgeable investor, neither a beginner nor an expert.

**_SmartMoney_ Online (www.smartmoney.com).** This isn't one-stop shopping, but it is darn close. It includes full mutual fund information, complete charting service, screens to sort stocks, and timely stories. If there is something else in the magazine that is not here, it may not be worth looking up. Pundit Watch is a favorite stop. *SmartMoney* keeps track of a dozen market prognosticators and calls them on their performance. For any new investor or longtime investor struggling to find some guidance from professionals, Pundit Watch is a reminder that you aren't all that far behind the professionals when it comes to understanding the market. The site also does a good job watching the economy here and abroad and dissecting the next hot investment before it's hot.

The *SmartMoney* Answer Center is the magazine's Q&A online. It's heavy on personal finance, but a bit light on investing outside of retirement planning with IRAs and 401(k) plans.

### *Worth*

*Worth*, another 1990s entry in the personal finance magazine arena, is the most eccentric and perhaps one of the more writerly of the major finance magazines, swinging from offbeat topics like Marilyn Monroe's finances to a painstakingly compiled list of the best financial advisers in the United States. Peter Lynch, the Magellan Fund guru, is the marquee name, though *Worth* often showcases other well-known mutual fund and money managers like Elizabeth Bramwell, manager of the Bramwell Funds, and Elaine Garzarelli, an independent New York City money manager.

***Worth* Online (www.worth.com).** At this site you'll find crisp reporting on the economy, with a recent cover story on the so-called new economy, which *Worth* says is real. Writers liven things up with the *Worth* Stock Challenge, now in its eighth year, presented in a fashion that allows you to test your picks against the professionals'. The site also features interesting pieces on how you can do important financial planning tasks better—like use state-of-the-art software to make mutual fund selections for your 401(k) or other retirement plan. This is also a good site if you're looking for a story that ran in a previous edition.

# BUSINESS MAGAZINES

Three major business magazines also provide news and insight on investing, several with enough coverage to make them candidates for your A list. Here they are in alphabetical order.

## *Business Week*

*Business Week* best serves readers who are working in management jobs. *BW*'s strength is its trend-delineating cover stories. For investors, the topics—from AT&T's challenges in a rapidly changing telecommunications market, to the future of China—give investors the kind of big-picture insights that can help you spot sectors you want to invest in, or companies in those sectors that fit your investment strategy.

 *Business Week* also focuses on investment topics such as retirement planning and how to play a bull or bear market. Its periodic mutual fund issues are as comprehensive as any other financial publication's and it publishes special mutual fund booklets for subscribers.

### *Business Week* Online (www.businessweek.com).
The *BW* web page is a miniature version of the magazine, perhaps the most attractive web site among those of the financial magazines. Stock and mutual fund tips, as well as tax advice, are the norm here. It also offers a comprehensive search service of scores of publications for a nominal fee. If you can't find it elsewhere and it's must-have information, it's worth it.

### Forbes

*Forbes* is essentially a portfolio of investment ideas—and profiles of dozens of companies an investor can use to pick stocks. The magazine can be hard-hitting, as it was when it lambasted *variable annuities* in an article in early 1998. The article was unsparing in its questioning of the value of these retirement savings plans.

> **variable annuities**
> annuities from which the investor receives a periodic amount of earnings linked to the performance of a portfolio of investments underlying the annuity.

But for the most part *Forbes* is a celebration of business. It does offer periodic coverage of mutual funds. For instance, an issue in late 1998 included analysis of more than 1,100 funds, but that's not even close to the size of offerings from other magazines like *Business Week* or *SmartMoney.*

**Forbes Online (www.forbes.com).** *Forbes* doesn't break new ground—or much old ground, either—with its web page. It provides a compilation of many of the stories in the current issue, a gathering of columnists, and its famous list of the richest Americans. There is a market update bar, which allows you to see how the various indexes are doing, but you can find that information on almost any major Internet access service, such as Yahoo! or America Online (AOL). There are also links to sister management-oriented publications *ASAP* and *FYI* and to *American Heritage* magazine, which it also publishes.

### Fortune

*Fortune* was created to appeal to America's upper management and it does that, though because the quality of the reporting, writing, and graphics is so high, it appeals to a broader spectrum of readers. The magazine has created a very decent personal finance section, which is as interesting as it is informative. Company and mutual fund manager profiles are illuminating. Investment selections have generally been on target. But this is probably not the must-have magazine for the beginning investor.

***Fortune* Online (www.fortune.com).** *Fortune*'s web page is a step above *Forbes*'s. It offers a compilation of current stories and a comprehensive career advice area called "Ask Annie." It doesn't have the focus or the depth of the *Money* web site, but then it's more an introduction to the magazine for nonsubscribers. You can also tap into *Fortune*'s lists, the *Fortune* 500 of leading companies and America's Most Admired Corporations. But for practical investment information and advice you're better off with *SmartMoney* or even *Business Week*.

# Measuring the Value of Newsletters, Brokers' Advice, and Analysts' Reports

More than a thousand financial newsletters make their way through the mail each day and crowd cyberspace, crowing about their authors' abilities to pick mutual funds, stocks, and bonds. More than two million investors read these newsletters, looking for investment advice and hot tips, in essence where to put money so it makes money. There is even a newsletter, the Hulbert Financial Digest, that covers and details the financial newsletters and reports on their performance.

Most newsletters tout a specific investment philosophy, either growth, value, momentum, or some proprietary methodology. Many of them have developed screens that kick out the majority of investments available to yield a short list of mutual funds, stocks, or bonds that are supposed to be the winning performers in the months to come.

## GOOD AND BAD NEWSLETTERS

Bear in mind that some newsletters recommend stocks they are being paid to recommend, and that trend is growing. In 1997, 42 complaints of that action were filed with the Securities and Exchange Commission compared to only 16 the previous year. Investors are pouring huge amounts of money into stocks and mutual funds, which accounts for much of the growth in newsletter fraud as cunning newsletter authors con unsuspecting rookie investors. The Internet is fertile territory for newsletters, which can be either without methodological merit or little more than covers for unscrupulous investors trying to manipulate the share price of stocks they own or are being paid to recommend.

Luckily for investors, not all newsletters are disreputable. Some can actually be quite helpful. *The Value Line Investment Survey* is a highly regarded report on investing. *Equity Fund Outlook*, which promotes growth stock investing, is a reputable publication that recognizes various levels of risk in devising its model portfolios, something a newsletter pushing an individual stock would never do.

But many miss the point, as well. According to investment research, the mutual fund portfolios recommended by investment newsletters averaged just half the return of the overall market between 1992 and 1997.

## The Draw of Newsletters

Why are they so popular? It is one more way to learn about investing, learn about stocks and mutual funds you might like to buy, and gather information on market trends. Most newsletters also create model portfolios based on whatever market strategy they espouse.

Truth be told, most investors eventually wean themselves from newsletters after they have devised an investment strategy. They take more pleasure in doing their own research, screening investments, and selecting stocks and mutual funds. For those just getting started, however, some newsletters are worth a look.

Here, then, are seven of the more veteran newsletters to consider. Get a sample copy of as many as you think interest you. If you have the time and interest, go to the library and read half a dozen issues to decide whether the strategies and portfolios being recommended are good fits for you. Feel free, too, to strike out on your own if you find others that interest you or fit your own investing philosophy more.

**Hulbert Financial Digest.** This is a great place to start, because *Hulbert*'s role is to assess the other financial newsletters. It will help you sort the decent newsletters and investment strategies from those that are mediocre or just plain wrong. If a newsletter doesn't appear in *Hulbert*, steer clear of it. It might be one of the growing number of letters designed to tout stock so insiders can make a buck on their shares before they dump all they own and send investors' shares plummeting. For a sample or subscription ($59 a year), call 888-485-2378.

**Equity Fund Outlook.** This momentum-style newsletter offers technical interpretations and a constant screening of funds. But its editor, Thurman Smith, isn't always right. In 1997 he warned readers that a bear market was on the way. So far, he's been wrong.

Nevertheless, *Equity Fund Outlook* offers scores of fund choices sorted by their risk profile, which can be useful to those in the early stages of identifying where their comfort level is. In a choppy market, especially, reminding investors of the value of matching risk tolerance with investments is a positive thing. For a sample or subscription ($125 a year), call 617-536-3842.

**No-Load Fund Investor.** Sheldon Jacobs's newsletter offers portfolios for a variety of investors in various life stages. He dishes up portfolios for young, middle-aged, and older investors, and for those who want to invest in a single fund family. Among the latter, he offers selections from Vanguard, T. Rowe Price, and Fidelity. For a sample or subscription ($129 a year), call 800-252-2042.

**Independent Adviser for Vanguard Investors.** With so many investing options and such a strong performance record, it is no wonder Vanguard merits its own newsletter from former journalist Daniel Wiener. The newsletter helps you sort through Vanguard's full plethora of index-based and actively managed mutual funds. It also provides insights into different funds' and managers' strengths and weaknesses and historical performances, and what you can expect from different funds in different types of markets and economies. The newsletter also provides the tools needed to devise a portfolio suited to your investment plan. For samples or a subscription ($199 a year), call 800-211-7641.

***Fidelity Insight* and *Fundsnet Insight.*** The former of these paired newsletters is targeted at Fidelity funds investors, the latter for those who use Charles Schwab, Jack White, or Fidelity Discount Brokerage. The newsletters provide insights into how these organizations are run, what their investment policies are and how they work, and which offer lower fees and better service; and they make recommendations from the fund offerings for various portfolios. For samples or subscriptions ($177 a year each), call 800-444-6342.

***Louis Rukeyser's Mutual Funds.*** The popular host of *Wall Street Week* hovers over this mutual fund newsletter by writing short introductions to a half-dozen or so brief stories on a variety of fund managers, investment strategies, and market and economic conditions shaping the current investing climate. He also includes his Rukeyser 100, a list of the best-performing funds for each month. The "Personal Planning" column on the last page offers advice on what to do with all the money you're supposed to make following the newsletter's tips. For a sample or subscription ($99 a year), call 800-892-9702.

## MORE INFORMATION: WHAT YOU CAN STILL LEARN FROM BROKERS

These are interesting times for stockbrokers. The ground is being dug out from under them as a result of investors' instant access to the Internet. With so much research available for free online and on the newsstands to any investor who makes the effort needed to find it, much of what brokers have argued for years that they add to the investment process no longer holds water. You've probably discovered much of this truth already from your own preliminary research.

But brokers still have something to offer: their own expertise and the research that is produced by their brokerage firm's analysts. This research may or may not be available online. But it can be valuable to you, especially if you are not inclined to make the Internet your second home, or if you prefer dealing with a person when seeking advice on your investing and retirement planning.

### Why Brokers Do What They Do

Remember, however, that brokers are salespeople. That's the first thing you should know about them and the last thing to think about before you act on a broker's recommendations. They make their living on commissions from the sale of stocks, mutual funds, and annuities. You meet them coming and going in your investing— first when you buy and again when you sell. Their commissions, however large or small, are deducted from your investment and reduce your total return. They are understandably prone to pushing products with the highest commissions. That often translates into investments that may not be a good fit for you or those that have substantial risk. Don't invest with anyone without double-checking that broker's recommendations first and without understanding all costs and risks associated with the investment.

That said, plenty of investors consider their brokers to be trusted advisers. That's increasingly common now that brokers are moving into personal financial planning, which is supposed to be designed to match your investing to your needs. And because brokers know you won't keep your money with a broker who makes bum bets, many are trustworthy individuals who have developed long-term and rewarding relationships with their clients.

Check with those clients—the broker's references—as part of your investigation into whether a broker is a good fit for you.

Traditional full-service national brokers such as Merrill Lynch and A. G. Edwards offer a wide range of services and financial products. Regional brokers such as Piper Jaffray in Minneapolis also sell a variety of services, and offer expertise in regional stocks.

### What You'll Get for Your Money

What you get for high commissions and sometimes a variety of seemingly niggling fees is, first and foremost, advice. Your broker will call with investing opportunities he or she thinks might fit your investing strategy. This won't be a good fit for you if you're a do-it-yourselfer or if you don't understand the products being offered to you. You'll have to do your own research first.

But if you do sign up with a broker, you'll have access to the research reports the brokerage creates in the course of making its recommendations. Those reports, often ponderous and data heavy, are the products of the brokerage's research department. Big brokerages can spend millions each year on these reports. They are circulated to brokers and other investment professionals, though increasingly you find them free or available for sale on the Internet. You won't find them in your local library, though you may be able to pick them up at a local brokerage sales office.

## ADVICE AND ANALYSIS

The analysts' reports cover a broad range of investment products from stocks to bonds to mutual funds. The reports are a mix of statistical data on the company and sector performance and commentary from the analysts on the company and its outlook.

A recent Morgan Stanley report on asset management and brokerage stocks illustrates what you can glean from a typical brokerage report. The report includes nearly two dozen stocks that Morgan Stanley follows in the financial sector. The asset management section of the report includes analysis on mutual fund companies, brokerages, and companies that sell insurance and annuities. What they all have in common is that they manage assets for institutions, corporations, and individuals. Among them are familiar names such as Charles Schwab, Merrill Lynch, and T. Rowe Price.

Typically, the report begins with an overview of the sector and the economy. Read it; it is important to know the financial water in which your investment floats. The analyst can tell you, for instance, that the sector has had a long run of high growth, as was the case in one asset management report. But, with costs rising because investors are pulling their money out of these stocks, the sector could be facing a downturn as a result. You can use that information to make a top-down assessment of how much of your portfolio you want to keep invested here.

Focusing on an individual company among the companies the analyst follows or researches, you find more cautious news. Stocks trade within a range that technical analysis can quantify over time. This stock is at the low end of that range, due mainly to market conditions. Value investors will perk up at that news, and the analyst acknowledges this as a would-be buying opportunity but then notes the sector's problems as a warning that this stock may not yet have seen its worst days in this economic cycle.

The analyst's next words are a reminder of just what this analysis business is all about: "We still believe [earnings] estimates and sentiment need to come down, but when that does happen there will be a lot to get excited about."

## Reading between the Lines

Never, ever abandon the notion that in time your friendly broker will call with this analyst's "strong buy" recommendation. That simple little sentence about the potential for excitement is all but meant to be read by a broker to a client. For you, however, this neutral rating means you should give thought to selling the shares. In fact, for many investors anything an analyst says short of "buy" is a recommendation to sell. The only thing holding back the broker and the analyst from saying to sell is the knowledge that many clients perceive a sell order as tantamount to admission that buying this stock was a mistake.

Leaving the front page of the report takes you into the solid background and analysis that is what you came looking for. For the asset management company under examination, the challenge is to keep nervous investors from cashing out of their mutual funds and other investment vehicles. It is the broad range of products that holds the key, the analyst says, and predicts the company will boost its offerings so an investor wary of the stock market can find bonds or other company-sponsored places to shift assets.

## Explaining How Industries Work

More industry analysis serves to educate you on how mutual funds make their money. Most of their profit comes from fees to manage your money. At the same time, load funds sold by brokers charge investors a commission, which gets passed on to the broker for his or her services. But collecting the money from you sometimes comes not at the beginning of the process when you invest in the fund but at the end when you sell.

These fees are called *back-end loads* or contingent-deferred sales loads. Trouble is the brokers must be paid whether the mutual fund collects the fee from you at the beginning or the end. A volatile market makes for volatile fees. This mutual fund company, already struggling with the expense of hiring hundreds of temporary employees to handle the volatile market, is also faced with huge fluctuations in its cash flow.

Now you can see why this is not necessarily a buying opportunity: This stock looks to be an underperformer for some time yet before the company gets its problems solved.

 **back-end loads**
also called contingent-deferred sales loads, these are commissions that get passed on to brokers, which you pay when you sell your investment in certain mutual funds.

The remainder of the report is a statistical field day of comparisons of revenues, expenses, operating income, earnings per share, dividends, and book value. The list runs to some 30 categories. The role of this information is, of course, to plot trends. Strong growth shows up in earnings per share growth forecast out five years, a typical and accepted period beyond which the numbers are mostly meaningless.

Here you can see in percentages and computations what the analyst described up front in the report: slowing growth in the short term; flat growth in the near term. If you're looking for proof of the hypothesis that this stock is a pass for now, it is there in the numbers.

# Chapter 11

# The Big Hitters: Morningstar and Value Line

B efore Morningstar. . . . It's hard to imagine mutual fund investing before Morningstar, though it
has been in existence only since 1984. That's
when founder Joseph Mansueto published the first
*Morningstar Mutual Fund Sourcebook* on mutual fund
performance. Mansueto aimed the publication at individual investors, professionals, and institutions. Using a
simple five-star rating system, he set out to grade mutual funds. Since then he has added stock and variable
insurance investment information. Today the sourcebook offers analysis and commentary on about 1,700
mutual funds.

It has, as one *Newsweek* article noted, democratized
investing. Its greatest strength is that its analysis and
rankings enable individual investors to quantitatively and
qualitatively judge the funds they are considering.
Granted, its five-star rating system has been criticized for
being too simplistic. But by using analysis to award five
stars to the top 10% of performers in each of a number of
mutual fund categories, then grading funds down from

there, it revolutionized how fund performance was perceived by investors.

## WHERE THE MONEY GOES

However simplistic the rating system may be, today most new money coming into the more than 8,500 mutual funds flows to those funds that have four- and five-star ratings from Morningstar.

Morningstar dominates fund assessing, and its now vast databases offer a comprehensive source of information on performance, portfolio, and management of more than 8,500 funds. Morningstar's commentary on many funds provides added insight into how managers perform. Morningstar also classifies funds according to their portfolios, not their prospectuses. Instead of calling a fund aggressive growth, Morningstar has devised a grid that goes from value to growth, from large cap to small cap, and based on an analysis of the portfolio pegs the fund to the appropriate block in the grid. As an investor, you'll find that differentiation critical to picking funds that match your strategy and asset allocation.

## HOW MORNINGSTAR WORKS

Morningstar uses fundamental analysis such as financial strength and earnings growth as well as proprietary formulas to analyze a fund's holdings. The five stars come on the simplest of grading patterns based on performance, risk, and costs. The top 10% of funds get the coveted five stars. The lesser ranks are divided similarly. (See box.)

### What It Can and Can't Do

Bear in mind when you consider the star system that it has pitfalls and drawbacks. It is, first and foremost, a

---

**The Morningstar Stars**

Here's what each of the Morningstar ratings signifies:

✔ *Five stars.* These are the top 10% performers with significantly above-average returns.

✔ *Four stars.* Still big winners, four star rankings include the next 22.5% of performers.

✔ *Three stars.* Average returns are represented in this group of the next 35% of mutual funds.

✔ *Two stars.* Laggards, at least for the present, are in this next 22.5% of mutual funds.

✔ *One star.* The bottom of the heap, these are the lowest 10% of mutual fund performers. These funds may suffer poor management, or simply be severely out of favor for the present.

---

measure of past performance, as president Don Phillips has noted repeatedly. It is a way to narrow the field to funds with strong track records. Morningstar itself does not tout it to be a predictor of the future. Phillips says it should be used as part of an overall assessment process that takes into account your investment goals and taste for risk.

Regarding the latter, the star system rewards momentum-style investing, which can be volatile. This is especially true for aggressive growth funds that can nose-dive quickly if the portfolio gets hit by a few high-flying stocks that will plummet in value if they disappoint Wall Street.

When you look at Morningstar reports, which are available in most city, town, and university libraries, check to see how long the fund has held its ranking. You want a long-term winner, not a fund riding the success of a hot sector, like banking funds did in the late 1990s, only to drop sharply in a year or two. And check out how much the fund has grown in size in recent years. Often a five-star rating comes on the performance of a relatively small fund. The five stars can draw hundreds of millions in new investment. And that, in turn, can change the style of the fund and affect its performance. Success, in other words, doesn't breed success in this instance.

And the star system won't help you search for value funds. Any fund in an out-of-favor sector is likely to have suffered on performance, for example, and with that have shed any stars it held in its better days. Also, remember that no matter how many stars a fund has, a high rating won't save you from manager turnover, which can leave you holding a bag of stocks picked by a now-departed mutual fund manager. Whether the brand-new manager can match his or her predecessor's record is anyone's guess—but it may be a gamble you don't want to take.

Morningstar's mutual fund information has traditionally been published in weekly reports that are mailed to subscribers, who include investors, financial planners, and other interested parties (including the mutual funds themselves). In 1997, Morningstar opened a web page that offers much of the same information (but not the commentary and analysis) without charge (www. morningstar.net).

## DIFFERENT WAYS TO LOOK AT FUNDS

The core print product is *Morningstar Mutual Funds* (800-735-0700, $495 annually), comprising detailed, weekly reports on 1,700 open- and closed-end funds that fund investors use to both quantitatively and qualitatively assess mutual funds. The monthly publication includes commentary on the mutual fund industry, on investing trends, and on individual funds as well. You can also purchase a no-load monthly report, called *Morningstar No-Load Funds*, which covers about 500 mutual funds for $225 annually. This is tons of information, and even as financial reporters we've sometimes found it to be tons more information than we've needed because it provides so much detail on funds we simply aren't interested in. But again, make up your own mind. Look at a copy of *Morningstar* in the library to see if the information is key to your investment decisions or a bit of overload.

As a light alternative, the *Morningstar Mutual Fund 500* offers information on 450 open-end and 50 closed-end funds and is published annually for $39.95. The best alternative, however, for those investors who are getting started in mutual funds is *Morningstar Fund Investor* ($79 annually), which looks at different types of funds, from large cap to high tech, and clearly shows readers which funds are performing best and why (sometimes huge, risky bets in volatile stocks are the reason and you'd want to know about that). The stock alternative for beginning investors is *Morningstar Stock Investor* ($79). See "Good News for Beginners" section for descriptions of both these publications.

## WHAT MORNINGSTAR REPORTS TELL YOU

The reports tell you how expensive a fund will be to own by covering specific expense information. Included are the *loads*—initial fees charged when you purchase shares in the fund, annual charges, and exit fees.

 **loads**
fees charged to you when you invest in a mutual fund.

The reports also describe the holdings in the fund, though be advised that the information on portfolio makeup can be several months old. It's important to get a sense of what types of stocks and sectors a fund manager has been using to get performance. But in a fund with high turnover—and many growth funds have turnover rates above 100%, which means they turn over every stock and/or bond in their portfolio at least once every year—the information on specific investments can go stale rapidly.

While you're checking out the portfolio, look at how the fund's assets are distributed by sector. It's an important insight into how the fund is betting on the market and how much volatility you may experience if you invest. A fund with 22% of its holdings in high technology stocks, for example, will generally have more volatility than one with just 2% or 3% of its holdings in tech stocks.

## GOOD NEWS FOR BEGINNERS

*Morningstar Fund Investor* is an unpretentious 48-page publication that offers more solid, useful information than any other periodical covering mutual funds without being ponderous about it. It's even lighthearted, and occasionally disrespectful when some fund manager or fund deserves a knocking. When the Astrologer's Fund announced an investment seminar program was "subject to change without notice," *Fund Investor* couldn't resist commenting: "We hope they can predict the market with more certainty than that."

The fundamentals articles are clearly written and thorough. A look at large cap funds in one issue took up only two pages—one of text, and one devoted to a table that dissected nearly two dozen large cap funds by holdings in the portfolio, P/Es, returns, and price valuation. The story was full of examples, the table full of insights on specific funds. Each issue also updates the Morningstar 500 list of leading mutual funds.

*Morningstar Stock Investor* is a sister publication aimed, as its title suggests, at stocks. Again, the articles are thorough and timely; there is commentary from other leading analysts and a market monitor showing leaders and laggards.

These are both fine publications full of first-rate information for investors, though the subscription rates for each are high, particularly when so much of the information not only is available for less money in financial magazines, but is free on many web sites on the Internet.

**How to Read a Morningstar Report**

Running about five pages, the QuickTake reports, which are available online or as part of the larger report series, can seem anything but quick when you see them for the first time. To simplify your perusal, we'll walk through a QuickTake report on Janus Twenty, a large-cap growth mutual fund with good performance. Its claim to fame is that it invests in just 20 stocks (as compared to more than 100 for some funds).

**1.** *Investment style.* It's right under the name and symbol at the top of the page. Here you'll find out what this fund is buying and selling. In the case of the Janus Twenty fund, a hot performer in the late 1990s, performance came from investing in large-cap growth stocks. These stocks drove the bull market from 1996 to 1998 so it's not surprising Janus Twenty did well. How well?

**2.** *Total return.* In "Snapshot," just below the graph showing how the fund stacked up against the S&P 500, the most widely followed measure of market performance, is the first round of performance stats for Janus Twenty. Here you can see when the fund lagged, paced, or outpaced the S&P. You want to know how this fund has measured up annually against the market. Is performance recent, or has this fund been a top performer for several years? Janus Twenty delivered uneven results in the early 1990s, when small cap funds were strong. It soared in the latter half of the decade.

**3.** *Return summaries.* In the "Risk & Return" section just below "Snapshot" you can find out what kind of long-term performance the fund has delivered on average. This is the meat and potatoes of picking a mutual fund because this is where the fund's wealth-generating power shows up. Janus

*(Continued)*

Twenty, for example, handily outpaced the S&P on average for a full decade. That's a powerful performance. But remember, that record came in fits and starts of big gains followed by lagging years. Invest in Janus Twenty and you may have to endure more volatility than with other, less concentrated funds in return for good performance.

**4.** *Risk.* You can see that volatility spelled out in black and white in the "Risk & Return" section where the standard deviation is reported. When it comes to risk or volatility, this is the number to focus in on. It will tell you how much riskier a fund is than its counterparts. In this case Janus Twenty, with a standard deviation of nearly 25, has the probability of experiencing 25% more volatility than its peers.

**5.** *Portfolio holdings.* You have to know what Janus Twenty's portfolio contains to understand its performance. Listed first are the top 10 holdings. Because Morningstar categorizes a fund by its portfolio, not its strategy or name, you'll find few surprises. The portfolio contains growth blue-chip stocks like Dell, Microsoft, General Electric, and Warner-Lambert. If you're online you can click on the stock symbol or name of a company and learn more about it and its performance in Morningstar company profiles.

**6.** *Portfolio summary.* Here you'll find how many stocks are in the portfolio. Concentrated funds like Janus Twenty will have relatively few stocks; in this case, and in contradiction to its name, Janus Twenty may own 20 or more different stocks. A big index fund tied to the S&P 500 will own 500 different companies. Small portfolios can often outperform large portfolios because fund managers and their analysts can more effectively follow the companies. On the other hand, some concentrated funds can be, as we have seen from the risk measurement (standard deviation), more volatile.

**7.** *Portfolio turnover.* Janus Twenty turned over its portfolio of stocks 125% in a 12-month period. The average big-cap mutual fund turnover rate is lower than that, around 85%. Many fund managers, particularly value-oriented star managers, pride themselves on low turnover. Remember that the advantage to you of low portfolio turnover can be a more tax-efficient fund. Nothing irritates investors more than to hold a mutual fund that not only performed poorly in a given year, but because of high turnover left them with steep capital gains taxes due.

**8.** *Sector weightings.* Funds invest in sectors of the economy, such as automotive, energy, financial services, retail, and technology. This section of the Morningstar QuickTake report will tell you which sectors of the economy a mutual fund manager has more of than others. Sectors go in and out of favor, some more frequently than others. Part of your work as an investor is to know which sectors are doing well and which are not. You can find sector performance information in many sources, from the *Wall Street Journal* to CNN.

In the late 1990s, Janus Twenty was placing its bets on technology stocks. That's not surprising news, when you recall among its top holdings are Microsoft and Dell—highfliers, to be sure. But technology is famous for its volatility.

**9.** *Asset allocation.* This is how a fund manager divides up his or her pool of money in different investments. Stock funds generally remain fully invested in the stock market. That's their strategy, after all. From time to time, cash builds up, either because investors pile into the fund faster than the manager can spend the money, or because managers are wary of the market and holding back. It's a tricky game, and plenty of managers pay dearly for trying to time the market. Asset allocation tells you how a fund manager is divvying up his or her cash.

(*Continued*)

In a bull market a fund with a lot of cash is hurting its total return. In a bear market, or in a market in the midst of a correction—a milder bear, if you will—cash can be kinder to investors, because cash, while it may lag great stock market performance, cannot rack up 20% to 30% losses like stocks in a losing market can. Having cash on hand is good for another reason as well: It gives managers the leverage they need to buy stocks at bargain prices.

**10.** *Manager profile.* It's one thing to buy a fund with a great track record, and quite another to learn the manager responsible for that performance left six months ago. When you check the manager biography section you can find out who the manager is and how long he or she has been there by looking under the subhead "State Date." Janus Twenty, we learn, is under relatively new management, though that management had delivered more than a year of good performance, albeit in a raging bull market.

**11.** *Fees and expenses.* In bull markets, growth investors argue fees are irrelevant if the fund is doing well. But bull markets don't last forever, and in bear markets high fees and expenses become huge hurdles for fund managers to overcome. You learned about fund expenses in Chapter 6. The example we're using here, Janus Twenty, is a low-expense fund, not charging an initial fee (up-front load), back-end load, or 12b-1 fees. The total expense ratio is 0.91%, which is below the 1.25% average for larger stock funds.

**12.** *Nuts and bolts.* Look here to find the minimum investment required to get into the fund. Minimums range from as low as $50 to mind-boggling sums of $1 million and more for big institutional investors. There's little sense in considering a fund you can't afford to get into—such as one of the high technology funds that requires a $10,000 minimum investment. One way around a high minimum is through an IRA. Often funds charge less if you are opening a retirement account. Janus Twenty has a $2,500 minimum for a regular fund, but only $500 for an IRA fund. It's worth noting that some brokers will offer lower minimums to attract investors. Brokers that offer the fund you're analyzing are listed in this section of the QuickTake report.

**13.** *News.* Check out this section online if possible, so you can click on any news stories that are listed about the fund. You can find background on new managers, shifts in investment strategy, and fund family news here as well.

**14.** *Profile and analysis.* It is puzzling that this is in the last section of the report, because it describes the fund's objectives. Bear in mind this is official, often boilerplate wording from the marketing and legal departments of the fund sponsor. As a result, it isn't always meaningful—which is why Morningstar created its own classification method and displays that up front in the report.

# THE LOWDOWN ON VALUE LINE

## *Value Line Investment Survey*

Value Line's weekly reports on stocks and mutual funds are a staple of professional investors' libraries. If you're interested in getting a sampling of the newsletter, you can find one there or in most public libraries. Samples and subscriptions ($570 annually) are available by calling 800-634-3583. Remember, however, that this is a reference service, like Morningstar's major reporting ser-

## How Value Line Ranks Mutual Funds

Value Line has two ranking systems, one to measure overall performance and a second to measure risk and other factors. The two are combined to create a ranking. Instead of stars, Value Line uses a numbering system from 1, the highest rank, to 5, the lowest. A ranking of 1 tells investors the fund they're looking at has made it into the 10% of funds that have the highest overall performance with the lowest risk. A 2 ranking applies to the next 20% of funds. A 3 ranking covers the middle 40% of funds that have average performance and average risk. Funds with a 4 ranking have managed to fall into the next 20% with both below-average performance and above-average risk. Value Line's dogs are ranked 5, which applies to the last 10% of funds, those with lowest average performance and highest risk.

For insight into how and why some funds work and some don't, look for all of the same components described in the "How to Read a Morningstar Report" box earlier in the chapter. The particulars you should take a look at when scrutinizing a fund using a Value Line report include a fund's investment style and return summaries, as well as its holdings, portfolio turnover, and volatility.

As with Morningstar's rating system, remember that comparing funds from different categories (e.g., comparing large-cap growth to small-cap value) by their rankings is meaningless. Keep your analysis in the sector you are considering when comparing rankings.

vices. It would be like buying an encyclopedia to look up one topic. Some reports are also available online (www.valueline.com).

## How to Read a Value Line Mutual Fund Report

Value Line continued its familiar layout of its stock reports when it created its mutual fund reports more than a decade ago. In actuality, they also look a lot like Morningstar reports. Mutual funds are segregated by sector, such as blue chip or small company, in the weekly booklets that are mailed to libraries, professional investors, and other subscribers. Each section opens with an overview of the sector, which includes a 300-word narrative of recent events impacting the pertinent industries, and news and analysis about specific companies that are part of the underlying portfolios of the funds in the sector. You'll also get an economic outlook for the sector, which tells you if Value Line analysts think the sector and overall economy have a bright future or some storms to weather ahead.

In many ways these overviews are as useful to investors as the fund profiles themselves. Included are six boxes showing top-performing funds in the sectors for the past 3-, 5-, 10-, and 20-year periods.

There is also a chart of highest-ranking funds, based on Value Line's risk and performance rankings. This is a good first screen for mutual funds. Look for long-term performance, then check the names against short-term winners and losers. You want to be certain you aren't buying a fund whose day has passed.

Another chart in this sector overview shows how the sector compares in long-term performance to the S&P 500. Performance is both graphed and shown in numerical form so you not only get a visual impression of how the sector has stacked up to the benchmarks, but you also get hard numbers to use when you are allocating assets.

*Chapter*

# Television and Radio

**H**ave you noticed lately that couch potatoes don't get as bad a rap as they once did if they're watching investment-related news? Unfortunately, though, as with any good thing, too much is bad. And there is just an unbelievable amount of business news to choose from.

Hand-in-hand with the growth of the Internet, investors have seen cable and commercial television just explode with financial programming. CNBC, CNNfn, and MSNBC are among the cable offerings investors can watch, though it is CNBC that devotes nearly all of its broadcast day to business-related topics. CNN *Headline News* includes business news as a part of each 30-minute news program. PBS and other publicly supported channels also produce business programming.

This endless stream of electronic information appeals to some investors because it gives them the feeling of being in the midst of the trading floor and gets them closer to the fever of a moving market. With viewer call-in programs, investors can find themselves talking to top Wall Street analysts, fund managers, and strategists.

Some of these shows also allow you to follow the

tickers of your favorite stocks. In the midst of an astounding market for Internet stocks, just seeing shares of a company bound upward by geometric multiples over the span of a few days can be intoxicating.

## HOW MUCH TIME DO YOU HAVE?

Unfortunately, watching television can burn up time you don't have. And even if you just play it in the background, like an easy-listening radio station, as you scan the papers or the Internet for financial news you can use, it can still be a little distracting sometimes.

All this nice-to-know information can amount to a lot of, well, noise. Like C-SPAN it can be hypnotic and addictive as it draws you into the ebb and flow of an investing day. You'll thrill to market rallies and wince along with the commentators when a stock tanks. Breaking news can bring a halt to your trading day.

In reality, financial television is a crazy mix of entertainment and information that can tap a viewer's deeper desire to be a professional investor. If you find you are drawn into investing as more than a means of retirement planning or funding your kids' college educations, financial television will undoubtedly become must-watch TV.

Or maybe you'll put a meter on your viewing time, much as you might do with your children's television watching or their allotment of cartoons. One or two hours a week of business news, divided among a handful of shows you regularly watch, should provide you with everything that television can offer a home investor.

## FINANCIAL PROGRAMMING WATCH LIST

### *Programs*

If your interest grows, you can expand your research time in front of the tube. Whatever level of interest you bring to the couch, here are some programs you should consider for your own watch list. We've ranked them, as is appropriate with any discussion of television, by how well they serve investors.

1. *Wall Street Week* (PBS).
2. *Moneyline NewsHour* (CNN).
3. *Nightly Business Report* (PBS).
4. *Business Tonight* (CNBC).
5. *Stocks to Watch* (CNBC).

**Wall Street Week with Louis Rukeyser.** If you're unfamiliar with Rukeyser, he's the dapper silver-haired dean of Wall Street commentators who has been weighing in on PBS on Friday evenings with commentary and the opinions of a handful of prominent Wall Street types for more than a quarter of a century.

Rukeyser knows the markets and is well prepared for the program. He speaks knowledgeably on bonds, stocks, international investing, interest rates, the business climate, and even politics. His influence and insight are evidenced by a guest list drawn from the upper echelon of Wall Street, albeit with the occasional rising star added to the mix for variety. Frank Cappiello, a Wall Street investment house manager, is the most familiar guest. He's a plainspoken foil to the more imposing Rukeyser.

It is from the likes of Cappiello, however, that you get a sense of the institutional caution Wall Street's veteran investors bring to the table—a sense that you do not usually find in hot mutual fund managers who still have powder burns on their palms from pulling the trigger on stock transactions. For any investor, personal knowledge of a down market is a critical balance to the heady can't-lose attitude the bull market of the 1990s has created. Rukeyser has a knack for putting his guests at enough ease to be cautious about the market on the air.

At the same time, Rukeyser is a reminder that investing should be rewarding, even fun. If he strikes you as a little too dapper and a little too smooth, overlook it. No one else on the airwaves is as capable of explaining the market in a way that both appeals to the experts and is still comprehensible to individual investors. He's also an asset when the market is in turmoil and you've got a nervous stomach to match. Rukeyser has a way of reminding investors that despite the uncertainty of the markets, this is a game in which the overall odds are stacked in your favor. His message is simple: In the long run, following accepted investment principles, you aren't likely to lose.

***The Moneyline NewsHour with Stuart Varney and Willow Bay.*** Varney and Bay talk business and investing (CNN weekday evenings), seeking to get behind the headlines with interviews with leading company executives as well as those who shape our perceptions of investing success (Dow Jones Industrial Average CEO Carleton Fiorina was a recent guest). This show's a good primer for understanding what creates company success and failure.

***Nightly Business Report.*** One weakness of television business programs is they try to pack too much noise and data into their allotted half hour. Even committed viewers can quickly lose their place or become distracted when company earnings reports are streaming from the mouth of the commentator. Rather than listening to seemingly endless paragraphs of performance, company by company, you might better go to the *Wall Street Journal* or the *New York Times* and pick among the articles you want to read.

Alas, overkill is the problem with *Nightly Business Report* on PBS. Dapper but portly Miami-based anchor Paul Kangas has both the vocal cords and dexterity to deliver the news; it is just that there is too much of it. The show is further bogged down by too many graphics and bits of data, made all the more distracting because it is scattered over the screen.

All is not lost on the *Nightly Business Report*, however. Its coverage of big stories and its company profiles, done in the comfort of noncommercial television and thus less mindful of time constraints, are thorough and comprehensible.

**Business Tonight.** CNBC's Sue Herera is perhaps cable business news' best-known female anchor. She comes off as knowledgeable and erudite without the stuffy insider quality many of her colleagues exhibit. The pace of the show is brisk, but not breathless. Herera also manages to stay away from lots of numbers.

**Stocks to Watch on CNBC.** This is stream-of-consciousness investing. You get a running ticker at the bottom of the screen and boxes of data on the side. In the middle you get market watcher Joe Kernen. Kernen has to be seen and heard to be believed. He is literally studying his own information screens, calling up stock symbols and commenting on what he finds—all while he is on camera. He is so completely untelevisionlike that he will ask viewers to call in with the correct pronunciation of a given company's name if he doesn't know it.

Along the way you'll also get to call in to chat with fund managers and market strategists who make regular appearances on the show. Day traders may find the market's moves as reported on this cable network of some value. But overall, it's less useful for beginners than, say, Rukeyser's *Wall Street Week*, where there is time between shows to consider the big picture and offer some context for the week's headlines. Watch CNBC when there is breaking news—for example, about corporate earnings, the stock market, or Federal Reserve Board actions.

### Networks

**MSNBC.** You'll be hard-pressed to spot the MS (as in Microsoft) in MSNBC. In its early days, the network made a pretense at being an amalgam of the giant software maker and Internet portal operator and the NBC network. That all but vanished in a short time, though, so that now the network is essentially one more 24-hour information service like CNN, though more focused on politics than business.

**ABC, NBC, Fox, and CBS.** The major commercial networks' commitment to business news is less useful to investors, though you should be watching at least one evening news broadcast to remain informed. Most times, the news is pegged to the economy and won't contain the kind of specific information you need to make investment decisions. For instance, the fact that Microsoft dukes it out with the federal government over antitrust issues makes a good network news story, but it doesn't tell you how the stock did that day, what analysts' earnings estimates or concerns are, or how many have buy or sell recommendations on Microsoft stock.

The network morning talk shows play an inconsistent game of investment news. Sure, they'll bring on celebrity investors, but they appear regularly for a time and then seem to disappear. Personal finance and investing book authors also make the rounds, as does the occasional chief executive officer (CEO). But if it's business and investing news you're after, tune in where that's all there is or you'll be watching Martha Stewart make Easter eggs rather than finding out how the Japanese stock market is doing.

The chief problems are time constraints and the often genuine lack of interest or knowledge of investment issues that seems to plague these shows' hosts. It simply takes the knowledge of a Rukeyser or Herera to move any conversation not only forward but deeper into a financial issue.

# Chapter 13

# Annual Reports and the Rest of the Mail

You like paper, you say? Then all you have to do is invest in a mutual fund, a stock, or a bond. You'll get plenty of paper. The reason behind the flurry of mail you'll start receiving, believe it or not, is investor protection. Institutions are required by the Securities and Exchange Commission to regularly report their operating strategy and their financial performance to investors. As a result, you'll get annual reports, quarterly reports, an occasional letter, and maybe even a regular newsletter (and that's on top of the performance reports you'll receive either monthly, quarterly, or annually, depending on how often, if at all, you buy new investments with the company). As a shareholder, you'll also receive letters to alert you to performance and management changes, as well as proposals to alter operating procedures and investment strategies.

While you might be tempted to toss these reports and letters in the trash along with your junk mail—don't. They're an important part of monitoring your investments, which is as integral to your success as buying investments in the first place. Written communications from companies can often be eye-openers, reminding you of some of the practical investing rules that sometimes even the best investors forget. In other words, investor

---

**Using Company Communications to Monitor Your Investment Style**

Here are some of the investment decisions that company communications will help you to revisit and monitor.

✔ Why you invested with a company in the first place.

✔ How thoroughly you did your investment research and what it told you.

✔ What you missed in your research.

✔ What you purposely overlooked in your research, especially if it has now come back to haunt you.

✔ Whether a company or mutual fund is doing what it said it was going to do or is switching strategies midstream.

✔ Whether actual performance is matching up with what a company is telling you.

---

communications should underscore investor basics and be reminders that allow you to judge and monitor investments and your own investment style.

What you discover will help you continue to refine your investment style and your actual investments. After all, investing is both an art and a science. The more you do it, the better you get.

Here are some fundamentals about the investment mail you've started getting or will be getting soon, along with some streamlined strategies for finding the must-read information in these investor communications.

## THE PROSPECTUS

Mutual funds are required by law to tell you what it is they're supposed to be doing and how well they've done it. That document is called a prospectus. Every ad you'll ever see touting a mutual fund's great performance will tell you at the bottom to get and read the fund's prospectus. For years a good many investors have managed to ignore that suggestion because of the mind-numbing verbiage funds managed to throw into the documents.

The news is that fund prospectuses are actually getting better and easier to understand thanks to the Securities and Exchange Commission's "plain English" rules, which require fund executives to communicate using—you guessed it—meaningful, concise language rather than legal boilerplate only a securities attorney can understand.

Since any fund you're interested in investing in will send you its prospectus (all you have to do is call the toll-free number), it can be a very good starting place for you to research or to double-check a friend's recommendation or what you have read in a newspaper or magazine. After all, doing your investment homework yourself will make you a much better investor.

## *What to Look For*

Here are the things you should look for and check in a mutual fund prospectus:

• *What does it do?* Look at the fund's basic investment strategy and check it against the fund's name. This will help you to understand what you're actually buying. While this may sound odd, the names of funds can be misleading, as can the broad marching orders, or investment strategies, some managers are given. The result may be you're getting more of what you might already have in your portfolio without knowing it. Case in point: Emerging markets mutual funds led the market in 1997, not because their managers were great world stock pickers, but because they invested huge portions of their portfolios in the U.S. stock market, which happened to be booming at the time. This was great for performance, but bad for those investors who already had large positions in the U.S. stock market and believed they were getting international exposure. This is also the section that will tell you what riskier investments, such as *derivative securities*, a manager might invest in to boost performance.

• *Financial highlights.* This part of the prospectus will tell you a number of things, including the fund's net asset value (NAV, as you'll recall, is the fund's price), total returns, and total assets. You'll be able to see if the fund's NAV bounced around over time. You'll also be able to see how the fund has performed; this is more important, especially with stock funds. Look at one-, three-, five-, and ten-year performance (or however many years the fund has been in operation). This will tell you if the fund has been a consistent performer over time.

• *Assets under management.* Why is a fund's asset size important? Because as it grows, its ability to find those hot investments and buy enough of them to make a dent in its performance diminishes. Put another way: Huge cash inflows into a mutual fund can sometimes, though not always, dilute its ability to hit home runs. In contrast to the fund that seems to be getting a bit slow as it grows, you should also be cautious about investing in a fund that has a dismal long-term record but has managed to do well for just a year.

• *Portfolio turnover.* Don't forget to check out the fund's turnover rate. As we've discussed, this will tell you how many times a fund manager sells his or her portfolio each year. Different types of funds buy and sell more or less often. For instance, S&P 500 funds that employ passive management (by buying what's in the index) should have a relatively low turnover rate compared to small cap funds, which by nature of their strategy will buy more volatile stocks. The real impact, however, is to your income taxes, since the capital gains taxes a fund manager incurs selling stocks are passed on to fund shareholders.

**derivative securities**
any financial security whose value to the investor is dependent on some other security's value and characteristics. Examples are options and futures.

**financial highlights**
a section of a mutual fund's prospectus providing you with net asset value, total returns, and total assets, as well as performance.

**assets under management**
the section of a mutual fund's prospectus telling you the fund's asset size, which is important in putting performance into context.

• *Expenses.* How much will it cost you to own a fund? Have fees decreased, as they should have if assets have increased? By reading a fund's "Transaction and Operating Expense Table," you'll be able to determine any additional fees a fund charges. Since it's easier to think in terms of what impact fees will have on your investment, the SEC requires all funds to show in dollars what it costs to own their fund for one-, three-, five-, and ten-year periods. The projection is made for each $1,000 of shares you own. This is also where you'll find the different charges a fund levies for the different types of share classes it sells. Some funds offer *front-end load sales,* which deduct their fee from your initial investment. Others charge fees every year—these are called *B shares* and the legal term for the charge is 12b-1 fee. Some funds also offer back-end load or C shares, which require you to pay a fee when exiting a fund. How long you plan to stay invested is the key indicator of which type of share you should buy. Even no-load funds charge expenses, though they're relatively small, since no one can operate for free. Expenses eat away at performance over time, so if given the choice between two seemingly equal funds, choose the one with lower expenses.

• *Shareholder services.* The *shareholder services* section will tell you the ins and outs of a fund. It will detail the minimim investment for regular accounts and IRAs, specify the minimum for additional investments, and spell out other options, such as whether telephone and wire redemptions require your permission in writing. If you want to use these features, especially any retirement withdrawal options, make sure to request them and sign the proper forms when you make your intial investment.

• *Timeliness.* It happens to the best investors, so make sure you check the date on the prospectus. They're published once a year and you'll want the most recent one. Somehow, though, old ones tend to get circulated, so be careful.

**front-end load sales**
a type of mutual fund that deducts its fees from your initial investment.

**B shares**
a type of mutual fund that charges you annual fees.

**shareholder services**
the section of a mutual fund's prospectus that details the minimum investment, methods of withdrawal requiring written permission, and so forth.

What's true of mutual fund prospectuses is true of all investment information: What you glean from a fund prospectus is most helpful when it's used in the context of comparison. How does the fund you're looking at stack up against its peers in terms of performance, turnover, and risk? As with any comparison, make sure to compare apples to apples. Comparing, for instance, a blue-chip mutual fund with a small cap fund won't tell you anything except that you're looking at two very different creatures.

Prospectuses are also published for new stock issues. If you're confident enough to invest in a company that's going public, read the prospectus to get a sense of who, what, how, and why the company deserves your dollars. Do you know what its competition is doing? Or how big or small its market is? The prospectus for companies going public is only the starting point of your research.

## THE ANNUAL REPORT

This is one of the chief communications tools for companies (beyond, of course, their actual performance). It gives them the chance to crow about good performance, talk about recent acquisitions or sales successes, and brag about new products, services, and markets. In leaner or downright nasty years, it also gives company executives a formal opportunity (beyond any negative stories that may have started appearing in the news) to explain their problems or at least try to minimize them by talking about all of the opportunities the coming year or decade holds. Then, of course, there are the financials, which should tell you how well the company did last year and how much it grew (or faltered) when compared to the prior year.

Most companies do a fairly honest job of telling the truth. But not all. That's why you should view what's said and what's reported with a healthy measure of skepticism. Companies use *annual reports* to put their

 **annual reports**
one of the chief communications tools for companies; should be viewed with some skepticism, as they are produced by the companies themselves.

best foot forward and have been known to spend as much as $25 a copy to do that as convincingly as possible.

Despite the glitzy photography and four-color spreads, annual reports can be deadly boring. But even if you're tempted to throw them in a corner of your office, force yourself to check the important points we're about to give you. After all, what you find in an annual report will tell you how well a company did. It's an important tool to use to assess whether your money is likely to grow if you buy the company's stock.

If you've already bought the stock, an annual report will tell you how well you did as an investor, not only in terms of the dollars you made—surely that's important—but in terms of the research you did to find the company and the judgment call you made to invest based on that research.

Here's a primer on the must-know annual report information you should look for.

### How to Read an Annual Report

When an annual report (also called a 10K report) arrives in the mail, it's your job to separate the sales job from the financial fundamentals to assess whether the company is in good shape or is floundering. Here are the key points to check out:

**Audited Financial Statement.** Even though it appears in the second half of the annual report, turn here first since the numbers will tell you how profitable a company is, how sound its current financial position is, and whether it's able to meet its obligations and debts.

✔ *Balance sheet.* Look first at the company's balance sheet, which tells you what it owns (assets) and what it owes (liabilities) at the end of the year. This of course is key to assessing how strong the company is financially.

✔ *Shareholder equity. Shareholder equity* is what investors own. It's what's left after liabilities are subtracted from assets.

**shareholder equity**
assets minus liabilities of a company—what all investors put together own.

✔ *Income statement.* This section shows whether the company's operations turned a profit or generated a loss during the year. You'll want to turn to the body of the report to find out what activities were responsible for the loss or gain and whether the trend is likely to continue.

✔ *Cash flow statement.* This shows the company's cash balances, after the costs of business activities are deducted. Does the company operate close to the edge or have adequate cash reserves to operate profitably through both good and bad times?

**Independent Auditor's Notes.** The annual reports of all public companies must be audited. Since auditors can be sued for providing assurances that are inaccurate, you can sometimes find hints or even outright admissions of problems in the *independent auditor's statement.* An unqualified opinion (which means that the auditor has found nothing to limit approval of a company's financials) asserts that the company has fairly and completely stated its financial position in accordance with generally accepted accounting principles. If, however, the auditor says the financials raise substantial doubts about a company's ability to continue as a going concern or identifies specific concerns, take note. That may even mean selling the stock.

**independent auditor's statement**
a section of an annual report in which an outside person who audited the report states an opinion; must be included by all publicly traded companies.

**Current Ratio.** Turn to a company's balance sheet and divide the total current assets, which are those that can be converted to cash within 12 months, by total current liabilities (those bills the company must pay in the next 12 months). You should get a *current ratio* of at least 1, which means the company has 100% of the cash it will need to cover all of its annual bills. Less than 1% and you probably want to rethink your investment.

**current ratio**
the total current assets divided by current liabilities of a company. The ratio should be at least 1.

**debt ratio**
current liabilities, long-term debt, other liabilities, and deferred income taxes of a company, summed and divided by total assets. A reasonable debt ratio is considered to be 55 or under, although some companies can handle a higher ratio.

 **profit margin**
net income divided by revenues. You can learn how well a company generates profits by comparing this number to those of the company's peers.

**Debt Ratio.** This measure tells you how much of a company's longer-term assets, like stores, offices, or equipment, are financed with other people's money. The greater the ratio, the more leveraged the company is. To calculate the *debt ratio*, add up the following four line items: current liabilities, long-term debt, other liabilities, and deferred income taxes. Then divide this sum by the company's total assets. You'll have to make a judgment call about the number you get. Some large companies with aggressive acquisition strategies can live with debt ratios of 70 or so and still grow and remain profitable. But unless they have a substantiated track record of doing that, stick with companies that have saner debt ratios, say of 55 or under.

**Profit Margin.** To calculate how well a company generates profits, divide net income by revenues. To find out how good that *profit margin* is, you'll have to compare it to those of its peers to see if the company is average, outperforming peers, or lagging them. Many investment services such as *Value Line Investment Survey* (800-833-0046) can tell you what the average profit margin is for companies in the industry you're investigating.

**Notes to Financials.** Don't skip the *notes to financials*, since they're the place where companies tell you about changes in the accounting practices they use to report company results. Changes should be viewed skeptically. If you can't figure out why the company is all of the sudden changing the way it computes or reports its financial fundamentals, call the company's investor relations department and ask why. Notes detailing litigation, risky investment strategies, and exposure to environmental liability are also deserving of a very careful read since these types of exposures can drive even good companies into long-term tailspins.

**Letters to Shareholders.** Read the chairman's letter after you have done the research just described and determine if it aligns properly. Company executives can sometimes be brutally honest in their letters, but more often they'll blow their own horn or hope their messages about prosperous futures will deter you from digging too deeply into the meat of the annual report.

### How'd They Do?

Now, after diligently reading an annual report, how well would you hope to do investing in the company? Are there any signs of promise or weakness that stand out? You can also use the strategy here for reading companies' *quarterly reports* (also called 10Qs), which companies use to update financial information and strategic and operating policies every three months.

## WHEN YOUR FUND MANAGER WRITES YOU A LETTER

Letters from mutual fund managers usually arrive only once a year. In a vacuum they might not be worth much, but if you've been tracking your mutual fund's performance these letters can give you insight into what your fund manager is doing wrong and what he or she is doing right. If it's been a gangbusters year, the letter might be a cautionary one, telling investors that the stock market doesn't only go up. Vanguard managers and executives did this repeatedly in the 1990s. If it's been a dismal year, hopefully the manager will be forthright with investors and explain what mistakes were made and how he or she hopes to break the losing streak. Robert Friedman, who heads up the Mutual Series family of funds, had the unenviable job of explaining why the funds had underperformed the market in the annual report the company published in 1999. Of course, underperforming the market is one thing. Racking up significant losses is quite another.

### When the News Is Bad

Of course, few events in investing cause more personal angst for a mutual fund manager than having to explain to

**notes to financials**
a section of an annual report that tells you about any changes in accounting practices of the company; also includes notes on litigation and so forth.

**quarterly reports**
reports companies distribute every three months to update information in the annual report; also called 10Qs.

customers how you missed one of the biggest market rallies in the history of the world. But in 1998 that was the fate of Brandywine Funds manager Foster Friess, whose funds lost a quarter of their value in the course of about a month. Not everyone was caught out in the rain. In contrast, Robert Stansky, the manager of the Magellan Fund, had the pleasure of explaining how Magellan had regained its footing in the market and turned in very acceptable returns the same year.

But Friess had a different story to tell. Known for his frankness, he used a letter in late 1998 to explain to investors and friends (since he has many who invest in the funds he runs) how his timing had been way off. On a hunch that the market was headed down fast, he sold a number of stocks. The problem was, he sold them too early, when there was still a good deal of upside to be had. Compounding his bad timing, he jumped back into the market right before it dropped sharply. The result was a 25% decline in the value of the mutual funds he manages. It happens. One result was that the *Wall Street Journal* pretty much dissected him in a front-page story.

Friess is not one, however, to shun the spotlight even if it's illuminating his foibles, and he acknowledged the story in the letter to shareholders a month after it appeared. What he had to say gave readers a sense that he was coming clean and taking responsibility for the errors in judgment. But he also went on to underscore the fact that anyone who can't afford to lose money ever probably shouldn't invest in the stock market at all.

"The article made us realize," he wrote, "that some investors may have expectations that we are not capable of fulfilling." But for shareholders who have received a number of these letters it was classic Friess reminding shareholders of one thing: He has a strategy that he continues to stick to because it has historically delivered outstanding returns. It involves getting in and out of the market at what he judges to be advantageous times.

"It is possible that you do not share our belief that being six months early is better than a day too late," he added, to drive home his point. "We want to be sure that our abilities are consistent with your expectations."

**Read Carefully.** Then he reviewed recent performance in the fund, noting that its strategy has once more delivered big returns, albeit to investors who joined after the fall in net asset value. He also quoted friendly press, in this case, a newsletter written by money manager Jim Cramer that also buttressed Friess's stick-to-your-strategy philosophy.

By touting the recent performance of the fund, he was not trying to regain favor with investors so much as remind them that his long-term strategy works. "While we aspire to more than just beating the average fund," he wrote, "these results do show your relative performance this year was solely a function of poor results for a single quarter when our disciplines kept us out of many stocks."

Granted, this is a letter written by one very rattled fund manager fighting to regain his place as a respected and respectable market watcher. Nevertheless, it shows the value of reading a letter to investors to help you understand what is happening to a portion of your portfolio.

Letters to investors are important for a number of reasons and Friess's is no exception. He used the letter to remind investors of several important tenets of investing and, more importantly, of his brand of investing. He also tells investors in no uncertain terms that the strategy they accepted in the beginning of their relationship with his Brandywine Funds is the one he is sticking with, no matter what the short-term setbacks are. He leaves nothing to the imagination. If you think his failure will impact the longer-term performance of the funds (and to put everything you're learning in context, you might look up the performance of the Brandywine Funds in the daily newspaper), he's basically telling you it's time for you to put your money elsewhere. You should hope that all of the people who ever have the opportunity to manage your money are as honest and have a strategy that they'll stick with in good times and bad.

## When the News Is Good

Let's turn now to the happier fund manager, Robert Stansky. Magellan Fund, the largest mutual fund in the United States, performed well in 1998 and into 1999 after several lackluster years. That gave Stansky the green light to use the fund's semiannual report to boast that he was beating his peers.

Stansky is a growth at a reasonable price (GARP) strategist who looks for companies whose earnings growth is likely to outpace the average earnings growth of the overall market. His 1998 investments included health care and drug stocks that pushed up Magellan's performance. But he also moved aggressively into tech stocks, taking advantage of any sharp drops in the sector to add to his holdings. Does that sound okay to you?

For one, it's a very specific change in the fund's holdings. But more important, it's a signal to investors that Stansky is taking Magellan into more volatile waters. Tech stocks like Dell and Microsoft can drive whole markets because of their size and their high levels of share price growth. But tech stocks can also bounce up and down like tennis balls right out of the can.

As you continue to grow your investment knowledge, the thing that will strike you about Stansky's letter, or other managers' letters in the future, is he doesn't acknowledge the additional volatility he is taking on: "At the end of the period, the technology sector remained among the most attractive in terms of its strong long-term growth and earnings potential." What about the additional volatility?

The closest Stansky comes to addressing the volatility of technical stocks is when he writes about risk overall: "Any number of factors can make stocks rise or fall over the course of a day, week, month, or even a year," he writes. "But over the long haul, it all gets down to one thing: earnings. Companies that can grow their profits significantly and whose stocks are fairly priced or undervalued have the best chance at appreciation."

That sounds plausible, reasonable even, don't you think? Do yourself a favor and check Magellan's performance in your daily newspaper.

# Going on the Internet for Information

I f the industrial revolution upended the early twentieth century, the invention and widespread use of the Internet knocked the last part of the century on its ear. It evaporated the barriers between the information available to entry-level investors and that available to brokers and professional money managers. In the blink of a few keystrokes, an investor today can determine what's happening to the price of a company, a mutual fund, or just about any market around the world—in real time. That means you can get the information you want or need right now, instantaneously, not when the newspaper arrives tomorrow or it's convenient for a broker or financial planner to call you back.

The lightning pace of the information the Internet makes available matches the pace of investment market changes themselves. The other word for market change, of course, is volatility. We've already talked a good deal about volatility, but bear in mind how the term translates in real life. The Nasdaq Stock Market Index, for instance, fell 5% in one day in April 1999 and the Internet was there to let investors know. Those who had online brokerage accounts could even access them to see what their specific losses were. Try waiting for some MSNBC anchor to tell you that. While investors are often cautioned that they could lose 20% or more in market turbulence, many have never experienced any loss at all, so this was a needed cautionary tale.

Of course, markets rise and fall and if you're already invested, the last thing you want to do is pull your money out when the market has slouched and you'll incur a loss. Most markets, at least historically, have always bounced back at some point.

If you're buying or selling for other reasons, however, you want to know the state of the market. Just as you don't want to sell low, you don't want to buy high, and the only way you'll know that is if you know how well the specific investments in question are doing.

It's hard to beat the Internet for gleaning up-to-the-minute information on an investment from the comfort of your office or home, any time of the day or night. Before going online for investment information became a reality for so many, do-it-yourself investors either could hope the markets hadn't moved too much from the quotes in the morning paper (which are, remember, based on prices as of the market close the day before) or could try to follow quotes provided by some financial news show as the numbers rolled across their TV screens, provided, of course, that they wanted stocks.

## ENTER THE INTERNET

Enter the Internet is right. As we write this, more than 54 million people worldwide go online for information, for news, to shop, or to socialize, and that number is increasing exponentially every day. From an information standpoint, there are literally millions of web sites on the Net that provide current and sometimes not-so-current information to anyone who searches for it. At the same time, there's been an explosion in Internet-based or online brokerage service offerings. "Technology is reshaping the securities industry as the meteoric rise in Internet-based brokerage firms demonstrates," says James Spellman, vice president of marketing and communications for the brokerage industry's trade association, the Securities Industry Association in Washington, DC.

How many people go online to invest? There were about 6 million people with 10 million online accounts investing through the Internet in 1999. More remarkable is the fact that almost half of all online investors began trading last year, according to Forrester Research in Cambridge, Massachusetts. Some experts predict there will be as many as 18 million World Wide Web–based brokerage accounts by the year 2001. As if that alone wasn't going to shape our markets in unforeseeable ways, the amount of trading that investors have started doing as a result of being self-propelled on the Internet is also skyrocketing. While traditionally the stock a company had outstanding turned over—was bought and sold—about once a year, today some companies' outstanding stock is bought and sold as many as 16 times over the course of a year.

## SO, WHAT IS THE INTERNET?

**portals**
servers providing usually unlimited access to the Internet through a phone or cable line, costing about $20 a month. Larger ones include AOL, MSN, and Infoseek, and often provide much financial information in an easy-to-find format.

Everyone talks about it. But what is it? The Internet is a vast linkage of computer databases developed more than a decade ago by high-tech gurus who saw an opportunity to take communication to a new level. You access the Internet through information *portals* using a telephone line or, more recently, cable television lines.

### Using Portals

Think of these, many of them whose names you've heard—such as America Online (AOL)—as the information highways you take to find the information you are seeking. You use portals to conduct searches or get to the Internet sites you want to visit. Many of these portals also offer their own information, such as mutual fund performance numbers.

Some of the most widely used portals include America Online, Infoseek, MSN, Quicken.com, and Yahoo! While much of the information available through the Internet is free, finding it is not. Expect to pay $20 or more a month for unlimited access that these portals provide. For new investors these portals are the friendliest introduction to the game. Sign up for one on a monthly contract and once you've accumulated enough web sites to satisfy your investment needs, you can drop the portal service and surf via a *low-cost Internet provider service.*

Also, remember that premium investment services offered by online operations like Morningstar and Quicken cost even more. For the sake of managing your money, manage the cost of your online expenses as well. Ask yourself: Do you really need to spend $100 a month on online information or would a good chunk of that money be better spent buying shares of a mutual fund or stock? Only you can answer that honestly.

 **low-cost Internet provider service** a connection to the Internet that is cheaper than one of the large portals, but provides less guidance; good for when you've become more experienced with the Internet.

## SORTING THE GOOD FROM THE BAD

Like that old saying makes clear: Too much of a good thing can be bad. The Internet may have made it easier for people who are interested in doing their investment research and even their investing online, but that doesn't mean getting to the stage of the game where we know exactly where to look and what to look at on the Internet doesn't take work.

One of the biggest challenges is narrowing your search. Using the Internet can be like going into a bookstore and pulling every investment and personal finance book, magazine, and newspaper off the shelves and stands and putting them on a single table. It would take you weeks—even months—to sort through them all meaningfully. And by the time you were finished, there would be an entirely new crop of publications to look through. The same is true of the Internet. The challenge for investors is finding the fewest sources of information possible that you can rely on for the information you need to make investment decisions and monitor those investments you already have.

If you spend time surfing the Net, you know that it is a time vacuum—not because it is slow, but because it offers so much information it's fairly easy to get lost in what you turn up. The trick in using the Internet for all it's worth is to manage both your time and the information it turns up wisely.

## STEER CLEAR OF SCAMS

Beyond eating up your time with information overload, there is another challenge to using the Internet: It involves steering clear of the slick promises being made by this century's version of snake oil salesmen. Instead of selling medical cures and beauty in a bottle, as they once did from the backs of their covered wagons, the slick salespeople of today are selling the promise of wealth.

Peter C. Hildreth, who heads up the North American Securities Administrators Association (NASAA), the Washington, DC–based umbrella group of state regulators, urged investors during a Senate conference in the spring of 1999 to ignore all Internet-based promises of quick riches, and asked them to delete all of the anonymous e-mail (also called *spam*) they receive that touts stocks and other investments. That advice is worth taking.

 **spam**
anonymous e-mail you may receive, often touting stocks and other investments. You should probably ignore and delete such e-mail.

At a minimum, be very skeptical of what you read on the Net. Ask yourself: If it's such a great moneymaking idea, why is someone telling 100,000 of their closest friends about it on the Internet?

## PORTALS TO THE INTERNET

Just a few short years ago online investing was unheard of. Now, it threatens to overtake the market of traditional brokerage houses. Because of the speed, breadth, and affordability it offers it is giving fits to those who are accustomed to being information gatekeepers and are used to charging for information and advice.

**Just Getting Started?**

You need an IBM or IBM-compatible personal computer with 8 MB of RAM, 6 MB available hard disk space, and at least a 486 processor. That's at a minimum. Most new computers have faster Pentium processors. You'll also need a Windows 95, 98, or NT operating system. If you have a Mac or Mac clone, be sure it has a minimum of 8 MB of RAM, 5 MB available hard disk space, and a 680 or faster processor. You'll need to select an *Internet browser* like Netscape Navigator or Internet Explorer and an Internet connection with a modem that runs 28.8 Kbps or faster (the newer, commonly installed modems generally have at least 64 Kbps connection).

 **Internet browser**
a software program that you use to access sites on the Internet.

You'll also need a telephone line (or TV cable line if you prefer to use cable), and access to a portal, which generally costs you a fee of between $10 and $25 a month. This fee may be tacked on in addition to the online time you'll have to pay for. Check around for the most reasonably priced online service and try to navigate one or more that friends use if possible before signing up. When you find one that's priced right and seems to fit your needs, you'll need to order the software and load it onto your computer. Once you do, the more developed portals will offer you Windows-style screens and icons or labels to click on. Click on the one that says "Internet Access" and you'll be on your way.

## Choosing a Portal

Most people will start using portals, the big electronic home pages from which they will launch their investment work. Because America Online (AOL) has the largest number of users by far, more than 12 million, it has a lock on newer Internet investors who use its expanded Personal Finance "channel" or site to begin searching for investment information. But MSN and Yahoo! also offer comprehensive personal finance channels to subscribers. Prodigy and CompuServe, once titans of the portal business, have faded sufficiently to move them from active consideration here.

All of these portals allow you keep track of your portfolio, read the latest business news, or check out the performance and particulars of a stock or mutual fund you like. AOL, MSN, and Yahoo! also provide links to a vast array of other Internet sites where you can find a universe of investment and personal finance information.

## ONLINE UNIVERSE OF INVESTMENT INFORMATION

You can stay inside the parameters of any of these portals or use them as launching pads to start surfing the Net. All you need to do is use the portal's search function or engine; type in what you're looking for—whether it's information on a specific company or on a mutual fund—and you'll be provided with a list of the sites most likely to feature the information you're seeking. You don't need to know every possible web site address under the sun. These *search engines* will dig them up for you.

### *Selecting the Right Search Engine*

Think of search engines as electronic card catalogs that find you web sites. They themselves are web addresses you go to on the Internet that in turn help guide you to sites you are seeking on the Internet. You enter a key word or words and in a matter of moments in most instances, back from the search engine comes a number of Internet addresses— sometimes a huge number of addresses. Think almost three quarters of a million addresses, which is what you can get if you type in a broad phrase such as "stock IPO."

You've probably heard of at least one of the best-known search engines, Yahoo!, the high-flying IPO of the late 1990s. Yahoo! was linked to America Online, but it now has its own full-service site; AOL uses Webcrawler as its search engine.

 **search engines**
these are tools of the Internet which allow you to, by typing in a word or phrase, retrieve all of the web sites that offer the information you're looking for and then some.

Here are four search engines you'll find useful:

**Alta Vista (www.altavista.digital.com).** Considered by many investors to be the best search engine available, Alta Vista also offers a breadth of information along with its search service and news from ABC News, in addition to electronic maps and people searches.

**Infoseek (www.infoseek.com).** This is a fairly familiar smorgasbord of information offerings including travel, computers, education, and breaking news. The personal finance section is comprehensive, much of it supplied by Microscoft Money Insider and Microsoft Investor. Reuters supplies the news.

**Webcrawler (www.webcrawler.com).** You can get an amalgamation of news, in addition to stock quotes on this search engine.

**Yahoo! (www.yahoo.com).** This is the granddaddy of all search engines, easy to use and linked to a number of news and information sources.

## What Can You Search For?

Any bit of information under the sun. Almost every company, no matter how big or small, is online. And many have extensive offerings, often free. Interested in some more mutual fund information? Search for Lipper Analytical, for instance, and you're offered the opportunity to visit the Lipper Analytical Services web site, or home page. This site will show you Lipper's top-rated mutual funds in a variety of categories.

Or search out Standard & Poor's and click on its web site. There you can catch up on how one of the leading stock indexes in the world is doing. That's useful in helping you determine how your large cap portfolio is performing in comparison to the index.

Search for Morningstar, click on its web site, and you can read columns written by its bright and knowledgeable online staff and check out the performance of just about any mutual fund or stock you can think of.

Or go corporate and search for IBM or Ford or Amazon.com. Most major corporations maintain fairly elaborate home pages on the Internet, offering everything from product and company descriptions to financial information and links to other corporate Internet sites. IBM will even sell you a computer on its web site, if you're so inclined. You'll find the same choices at Compaq, Dell, and Toshiba. And while Ford won't sell you a car or truck—yet—Amazon.com's very reason to exist is to sell you a book or compact disc over the Internet.

## ONLINE NEWS

Newspapers and periodicals also maintain web sites, called news sites, which can be rich sources of information, data, and access to the contents of back issues. *Business Week*, for example, lets you read some of the stories in its current issue or search through recent issues for the topics you're interested in. Newspapers such as *Investor's Business Daily* (www.investors.com) and the *Washington Post* (www.washingtonpost.com) also have extensive news sites, which give you today's news (or at least Mondays through Fridays at *IBD*'s site). Many state and local newspapers also have news sites, which often use national wire service stories to round out their business, economic, and market coverage. More newspapers are beefing up their investment sections, knowing that you and potentially thousands of other readers will come searching for news you can use.

While some newspapers, such as the *Wall Street Journal*, have closed their news sites to anyone who isn't a subscriber, sometimes the portal you're using offers a keyword service that allows you to access the publication you're looking for free and with great ease. With AOL, for instance, you're just a keyword away from the sites offered by *Business Week*, Morningstar Mutual Funds, and other news, analysis, and market tracking services such as Sage and Motley Fool. Hit the keyword button, type in where you want to go, press return, and you're there.

# THE BEST SITES ONLINE

We've said it before, and we'll say it again: There's more investment information than you'll ever need or use in your life on the Web. If you're a news and market junkie, surf until your heart's content and your eyes are bleary. But if you're somewhat normal, with family, friends, and a job, pick the site or two that are helpful to you, get what you need when you need it, then log off. The following list is not meant to be a must-browse offering. Just as different styles of journalism are more meaningful to some people, different web sites are, too. We've already told you about the news sites and what prominent sources of analysis like Morningstar and Value Line can do for you. Now it's time to find the web sites you can use to aid you in doing your investment selection homework. Many of these sites also offer a *screening* capability, which allows you to narrow your search to just those investments that meet your prerequisites.

**screening**
a search method that allows you to set parameters you want to satisfy in an investment, and then filters out investments that don't meet your criteria.

**Using Screens**

The better stock and mutual fund web sites offer screens. Screening is a technical search method, as the name infers, which allows you to screen for certain parameters or performance levels you want in an investment. When you hit "go," the screening engine will comb databases for stocks or funds that meet all of your criteria. Of course, it works by filtering out all that do not. Consider what's left the first cut in your search for investments. As an example, you can set up a web site screen to look for a large-company growth mutual fund that has 20% average annual returns for five years and below-average turnover without any tobacco company stocks. Or screen for companies in the health care sector with market caps of less than $500 million and 18% earnings growth for at least three years. Happy screening.

If you're hot on the trail of a prospective investment, these are good sites to search for news and info as well.

With those cautions out of the way, here is a look then at some of the more popular information and data providers you can access over the Internet and what you'll get.

## All the Bells and Whistles

**BigCharts (www.bigcharts.com).** Wondering what the price of a stock you're interested in has done over the past year? How about over the past month? This site offers some of the most meaningful charts available for free on the Web. It gives newer investors an up-close look at factors such as price appreciation, while more advanced investors can seek out charts that show multiple factors.

**CBSMarketWatch (www.cbsmarketwatch.com).** This is a full-service site with original news reporting, all the data you could ever use, market data and monitoring tools, and a portfolio tracking function. The columnists' accessible style is also attractive. Look for editor Thom Calandra's "StockWatch" columns first. Dr. Irwin Kellner offers a dose of informed economic analysis as the site's resident chief economist. The popular Frank Cappiello, a San Francisco money manager, also weighs in regularly with thoughts and stock tips.

**Investor Guide (www.investorguide.com).** Call this the beginners' guide to the investing galaxy, complete with an investment glossary and handy explanations of just about every type of investment under the sun. That's the focus the site is meant to have, according to founder Tom Murcko. Of particular use is the section on how to pick an investment selection strategy.

**Investor Home (www.investorhome.com).** This site claims it is dedicated to help educate investors invest appropriately by finding the right information. If offers portfolio tracking that allows you to follow, in a very readable report form, all of your investments in one place. At the same time, it offers real-time index tracking from the Dow Jones Industrial Average to the 30-year bond yield. You can get mutual fund and stock quotes, earnings estimates and analysts' reports, and links to a growing array of magazines, news sites, and online brokers. If you love this site, you can even make it your home page—for free, no less.

**Microsoft Investor (www.investor.msn.com).** It's interesting to watch how a half dozen investment professionals self-destruct on this site with hypothetical $100,000 portfolios. Watching a recent group (save for one) lose money was argument enough for careful investment selection.

The site is full-service, and its handy portfolio-tracking feature will alert you to news impacting any stock or mutual fund you hold. That's useful when there's a management change, breaking news, or updates on insider trading that could affect your holdings. Cost is $9.95, so make sure to check out the site's 30-day free trial before you sign up.

**TheStreet.com (www.thestreet.com).** Be careful with TheStreet.com. The reports and analysis will crush your e-mail queue with updates throughout each trading day. They're geared to the needs of day traders and market professionals more than they are to private citizens managing a long-term retirement portfolio. The site itself features all of the usual bells and whistles, plus a flashy lineup of homegrown news and features—cofounder James Cramer is present, but not overbearing It's a stock picker's paradise of data on new highs and lows, and other market movement. If you want a dose of Cramer, go to Commentary. Also look for senior writer Herb Greenberg. He writes for *Fortune* and appears on CNBC. No pompous pontificator, Greenberg acknowledges his record, good and bad, on stock picks investors call him on. Since TheStreet.com costs $9.95 per month, or $99.95 per year, check out its 30-day free trials to see if you'll use the crushing amount of info that will be dumped into your e-mail daily.

**Yahoo!Finance (yahoo!finance.com).** It's one of the Web's first directories, and, while it offers decent portfolio tracking, a plethora of Reuters news coverage, and real-time indexes tracking (including Nasdaq and the S&P 500), stock quotes are delayed, which in this world of instantaneous information and lightning-speed markets is probably something to avoid.

### Just the Facts, Please

Not all sites offer bells, whistles, news, or even portfolio tracking services. But if you're hot on the trail of a stock and need more information and research you can't seem to find elsewhere before buying, the following sites may be useful.

**First Call (www.firstcall.com).** This site bills itself as a real-time provider of company research, earnings estimates, and corporate information—five million equity and fixed-income reports and research documents all told, and growing. The company doesn't offer a free trial, but you should be aware that you can get First Call reports from a number of other web sites, so check your favorites first. Individual earnings estimate reports cost $1.50 to $9. The different levels of product and service offerings aren't clear on the First Call web site, but you can get the information by calling toll-free, 888-450-7439.

**FreeEdgar (www.freeedgar.com).** This site isn't jazzy—there's no breaking news per se—but it does offer investors free access to all of the SEC filings a company must make—including annual and quarterly reports. The reports can be downloaded, and the site also allows you to sign up for free e-mail alerts of targeted company filings by creating a your own watch list of stocks.

**Multex (www.multexinvestor.com).** Analysts' reports on stocks are often hard to come by unless you have a relationship with a brokerage doing research. And few of us have relationships with half a dozen brokerages, which is what you need to gather a respectable amount of analysts' research on a given stock. Enter Multex, an online service that will sell you research reports from a score of major brokerages. Enter a stock symbol and Multex delivers up a listing of current reports. When we entered American Retirement Corporation (ACR), for instance, we got 10 listings of reports that could be purchased and three that were free.

The reports aren't cheap, but considering the convenience and speed of access, the price seems minimal, especially if you trade only a few times a year. One to five pages are $10, six to 12 pages are $25, and on up to $150 for 60 or more pages. Be aware that analysts' reports will skew toward buy recommendations. That's the point of their work: to find stocks to buy. Be mindful of the dates on some of the information, which can remain on the site for weeks.

## ONLINE BROKERS
## AND FUND COMPANIES

Online brokers have taken to the Internet in droves, as have mutual fund companies. And they're all vamping up their web sites regularly with data, information, news, and handy calculators that allow you to see how well you're doing and how much you need to invest to meet your goals.

Of course, they're hoping to capture your business, since once you've set up an account with one of these firms, you'll be able to buy and sell mutual funds, stocks, and bonds online. If you're simply buying mutual funds in your 401(k) plan at work or want to purchase a few no-load funds through one or two no-load fund families, you probably don't need an online brokerage account.

If you expect or know your trading will be more extensive, an online brokerage account can be ideal. To purchase investments or make trades with an online broker, however, you will need to set up a money market account with them, so they can access your money when you make a trade. Before you do that, however, check out their wares—what they offer and at what price. Also be advised

**market orders**

an order for stock that tells the broker you will buy at whatever price the market is paying.

**limit orders**

an order for stock that tells the broker you will buy if the price of the stock is below a limit you set.

that there are two different types of stock orders you can place: *market orders*, which tell the broker to buy the stock you want at whatever price the market is paying; and *limit orders*, which limit the broker to buying the stock at the price you specify. With the price of some stocks changing quite significantly over the course of a day, limit orders are advised, lest unbeknownst to you your order for 100 shares of XYZ stock at $20 a share turns into an order of 20 shares of XYZ stock at $100 a share by the time your order is fulfilled.

Most of these brokers also offer a wide universe of bonds and mutual funds, though you should at least ask what the transaction fees will be on no-load mutual funds you can get a whole lot cheaper from the fund family itself. Of course, there is a lure to one-stop investing and record keeping. If your portfolio is growing to the point where you want one performance statement each month, not five or 10, by all means set up an account through one online discount broker.

Here's a sampling of some of the more prominent online brokers out there:

**Ameritrade (www.ameritrade.com).** This is a solid firm that is accessible for average investors and doesn't cater to just day traders. Wall Street research isn't included in the low commission structure, however, but the first 100 stock quotes you request are free and 100 more are free with each additional order you place. Cost: $8 market order, $13 limit order.

**Charles Schwab (www.schwab.com).** Schwab may be the biggest game in town, but it's also the priciest. However, there are a number of investors willing to pay the price for good customer service, best execution, and phone access to brokers should the online service shut down. There's decent analysis and good stock screening, as well.

**Discover Brokerage Direct (www.discover brokerage. com).** This brokerage is owned by Morgan Stanley Dean Witter and reflects its extensive retail experience by offering new and more sophisticated investors all of the equity research and quality information they could want at a reasonable price. More than 5,000 mutual funds are available, most for no transaction fee. (The fee is $25 for the few funds that do still charge one.) Market orders are $14.95, and limit orders are $19.95 up to 5,000 shares.

**E*Trade (www.etrade.com).** This firm came to widespread attention when its order-executing ability was pushed to a screeching halt several times in early 1999—overtaxed by day traders buying and selling Internet stocks. It has invested millions to correct its technical glitches and provides top-quality company research reports, albeit from one source: BancAmerica Robertson Stephens. Look for its stock-trading contests, which are fun to watch. Market orders cost $14.95, and limit orders cost $19.95 up to 5,000 shares.

**Suretrade (www.suretrade.com).** This broker offers a bare-bones approach to trading that is reflected in its trading prices. You'll get 100 free quotes a day (and we sincerely hope you don't use them all) and one more quote for each order. All trades cost $7.95 up to 5,000 shares.

**Waterhouse (www.waterhouse.com).** This is the broker that's giving Schwab a run for its money and its clients, thanks to its low price for trades. You won't get Wall Street research here, but you will find alternatives such as Standard & Poor's. If you don't mind fleshing out your research elsewhere, this is a fine place for your accounts. All orders cost $12 up to 5,000 shares.

# Chapter 15

# Hands-On Investing

If you're technically inclined, or required to use the Internet in your job, it's easy to imagine performing every bit of your investing online—your research, your trading, and your portfolio tracking. It's fast, accurate, and convenient. But it's not the only way. Plenty of very good investors don't go near a computer and still manage to do well with their investment plan.

After all, some very notable low-tech, high-touch investors have made millions of dollars for decades—starting long before the Internet was even a twinkle in its creators' eyes. Many still do. Whether you prefer to do it the time-proven way or zip online whenever you have a question, there's still much to be learned from a more hands-on approach. What you see, hear, smell, and touch can help make investing more interesting by engaging all of your senses. It can also alert you to new choices and help you narrow those choices you've already identified so you can put your money where you're most comfortable.

Here are some tips on how to make the most of this venerable and venerated approach to investing.

# GET YOUR HANDS DIRTY

With ink, that is. First off, you'll need a good newspaper. The *Wall Street Journal* or the *New York Times* are your best choices if you're inclined to buy a national newspaper. A big-city daily will often be just as effective. You need to track two things in your newspaper: business and economic news and data.

The news is how you learn about new opportunities and monitor the companies you already own stock in. The data is how you measure the value of your portfolio's financial performance. It's also how you size up the financial performance of potential investments.

Read the paper every day for continuity. Doing so is crucial to your understanding of the economy and the ups and downs in value of specific stocks. It's alarming to look at a stock that has fallen 10% and wonder what happened. Did the president fly to Mexico with the payroll? Did the company lose a lawsuit or report that earnings took a nosedive? Was there a leak about plans for a massive layoff?

This type of news is important because it could be a signal to sell if you've determined that the rest of the company's fundamentals aren't strong. But if the drop came because the sector overall has been doing poorly, you may see the fall in share price as a buying opportunity. In other words, you believe that despite the fact the sector is down, your company is as strong as the day you bought its stock.

Use the popular indexes published in the financial section to measure your portfolio's progress. The S&P 500 index is the most popular, but look too at the Wilshire 5000, and at any of the indexes that track the categories of investments yours fall in. They'll give an idea of how well you're doing when compared to the averages.

Don't forget to use the papers as a great tool for finding new investment ideas. Look for trends, such as the graying U.S. population, which you believe some companies are well positioned to take advantage of.

Once you've bought one or more investments, track their performance. Every weekday the major daily newspapers across the country will tell how your mutual funds, stocks, and bonds are performing.

## MINING FAMILY, FRIENDS, AND COLLEAGUES

Newspapers are only a part of the hands-on investing you can do. A network of opportunities surrounds you. Your friends and neighbors, your relatives, and your colleagues at work are all sources of investment information and potential leads on investment opportunities. We're not talking about hot tips or suggesting that you should jump at any idea someone plants in your ear. But if an investment someone tells you about sounds like it might have merit, by all means check it out and do some research.

You are tapping into the same network you would use to find out about a new job, a good restaurant, or a decent place to have your car serviced. Here's how it works. Simply ask someone how his or her mutual funds or stocks are doing. Sometimes people rave without really knowing what they're talking about. Maybe they don't know why they invested in a mutual fund in the first place, what the total return was last year, or how it's faring in a shaky economy. If that's the case, don't put too much stock in what you're hearing.

But if, on the other hand, they talk intelligently, by all means open up your own investigation and check out the fundamentals and performance you've learned to look for.

What are you seeking when you ask about someone's portfolio? The same things professional analysts and money managers look for: strong companies with a bright earnings outlook. They can be growth-oriented companies already on a roll. Or, maybe you're hearing about companies that have been hurt by some negative factor that has been corrected or soon will be. When the news becomes widely known, their share prices will rise. Analysts call these earnings surprises.

be among amateur investors willing to listen to you and answer the most elementary questions. Clubs average about 15 members, each chipping in less than $50 a month to a portfolio of about 15 stocks.

Members gather monthly to review their portfolios, report on analysis they've done on potential investments, and make investing decisions. If you are a member, count on performing a specific function for the club, such as following economic indicators or tracking a particular sector of the market. Analysis of particular stocks, bonds, or mutual funds also falls to club members.

To keep your place in any investment club, be sure to do your homework. You are a member of the club, a contributor to its collective wisdom, not the major recipient of every other member's hard work.

Most clubs are democratic—so the majority rules on investment decisions.

How well do they fare? Pretty darn well. Their average investment record is about even with professional portfolio managers. That means they beat the S&P 500 index about half the time.

Turnover in clubs is high, however, and some don't last very long. A couple of reasons for the failure: disagreement and fraud. It's hard to share investment decisions with others, especially if certain members feel strongly that an investment should be made, while others are opposed. Remember, an investment club is only a part of your life as an investor. You can still make outside investments and should.

Clubs, too, have been victimized and fraud can be a problem. In 1998, the Life Club of America was ordered to pay back $26 million bilked from investors. The club claimed to be an aid to minority investors but the court ruled it was little more than a scheme to bilk investors out of millions.

A computer software program devised by another investor in Colorado was said to be a way for club members to invest in stock options that would beat the S&P 500 index. Instead, it enriched the man who created the software program by about $400,000.

One way to check on any investment club you are considering joining is to ask if it is a member of the National Association of Investors Corporation. The NAIC says its member clubs are reputable. In nearly 50 years it has uncovered just 20 cases of fraud in member clubs. Most of those involved treasurers of clubs taking off with the money. Other times, money was siphoned off over time. You can avoid that situation by taking turns diligently checking your club's books, and by insisting that the treasurer bring all club records to every meeting.

Overall, investment clubs can be fun and rewarding. They give you a chance to talk meaningfully about your portfolio and about the market with others who have put their money on the table just like you. For more information on investment clubs or how to start one, contact the NAIC at P.O. Box 220, Royal Oak, MI 48068, or call 248-583-6242.

Joining the NAIC for a nominal fee gives you access to information on how to start and run an investment club. You'll also receive the association's magazine, *Better Investing*. You should also consider owning a copy of *Starting and Running a Profitable Investment Club*, the NAIC's guide to investment clubs. If you are on the Internet, you can find NAIC at www.betterinvesting.org.

## REMEMBER THE LIBRARY?

The library can be an important and economical place to research investments. There you can find *Value Line Investment Survey* reports on thousands of stocks and mutual funds. You should also be able to check out Morningstar's various reports on mutual funds and stocks. As you know, a subscription to either of these services could cost you hundreds of dollars and amount to hundreds of pages of analysis each year on hundreds of stocks or mutual funds you may not be interested in. The library is a fine alternative, especially if you're building a portfolio of long-term holdings.

Other periodicals you can read at the library can also help you find investment opportunities. Most libraries get *Barron's*, *Bloomberg Personal*, *Business Week*, *Money*, and *SmartMoney*. Don't overlook *Fortune* and *Forbes* for their profiles of companies and management.

Then, miracle of miracles, there are the books. Your stock holdings in big blue-chip companies like Ford, Kellogg, or Boeing should prompt you to read one or more of the major exposés of these large and well-known American companies. Profiles and histories of these and many other companies are published regularly. While you may not want to part with the $30 for your own copy, your library probably already has.

Autobiographies are also an important source of information on how American business works. The recently released *Direct from Dell: Strategies That Revolutionized an Industry* by Michael Dell (HarperBusiness) and *Guts: The 7 Laws of Business That Made Chrysler the World's Largest Car Company* by Robert A. Lutz (John Wiley & Sons) are two examples. Scores of corporate founders have published books on their business philosophy.

You can also find books on investing principles and success stories—such as best-sellers from Warren Buffett, manager of the millionaire-making Berkshire Hathaway portfolio. The library is also a great place to find out how Wall Street works, or where you can invest overseas. You may also be able to go online on one of the growing number of library computers for little or no charge and do your research that way.

Many larger libraries also offer some level of research to patrons for a small fee or no charge at all. You can ask at the reference desk for help on investment- or business-related research. Company reports, sources of stock market data, or investing newsletters are often found in the reference section.

The library is also a great place to find older articles about companies you are researching. Even online services cannot always offer you a story that ran, for example, three years ago. But a library may have a copy of the journal in which it appeared in its stacks, there for the requesting. And with many newspapers and other periodicals on microfilm, you can go back even further, and often see graphics and pictures that ran with the original story that are not available from online references.

Don't forget to use college and university libraries in your area, if your local public library is a little light in the investment and business stacks. Call first to see if the academic library is open to the public and expect to show a driver's license or picture ID. Yes, even libraries have cracked down on whom they allow in for security reasons.

Bookstores can be great treasuries of both news and investing styles. Many of them today encourage browsing by offering patrons comfortable chairs or even coffee bars where both books and magazines are allowed. It's a pleasant and potentially profitable way to while away an hour a week. Who knows? You may decide to buy a book or subscribe to a financial magazine as a result.

## DO YOUR OWN TIRE KICKING

Don't hesitate to visit the companies that interest you in your city, your county, or even your part of the state. You'll be joining the noble army of financial analysts, researchers, and mutual fund managers who each year visit scores of companies looking for growth or undiscovered value. You may not receive the kind of red-carpet treatment these professionals are accorded. But you can still tour the plant or the office, see the physical condition of the facility, talk with employees, and see some of the products a company makes.

Coupled with an annual report, which you can get from any publicly traded company, and your newspaper clippings and any other information you can gather from, say, your broker or the aforementioned investment club or friends and neighbors, you can begin to get a picture of your target.

Do you like the products but worry about the physical condition of the plant? That could be a sign the company is pumping everything into current production, or its profit margins are so tight there is no room for capital expenditures. Or it could be something of an entrepreneurial contrariness. Some smaller, newer companies pride themselves on spartan surroundings.

On the other hand, you could be looking at a company with a profound disregard for safety and efficiency. That Dumpster full of rejects could mean sloppy production or faulty design. Or it could mean a new product, under development, is proving cantankerous. The point of your research is first to identify the issues, then find answers before you invest.

Sometimes the picture you get may be too good for your comfort. You like the company but you're concerned that the lavish headquarters and the seemingly top-heavy management structure will sap the company's growth potential. Your hunch could lead you to discover the company isn't watching overhead closely because management is more interested in its own lifestyle than in its investors' money or its employees' productivity. Or it could mean a well-heeled company that knows that in order to attract top managers and employees it must offer attractive surroundings. Get the real story.

Obtain any printed materials you can when you visit. Tour guides, a company history, annual and quarterly reports, and analysts' findings are just some of the publications you should take. You're looking for all the information on this company you can gather, from product descriptions and company newsletters to financial information and press releases about winning products and services.

While you are there, learn about the full array of products and services. Sample them if you can. Peter Lynch, the famous Fidelity Magellan Fund manager, was fond of promoting the image of buying those products he himself used and liked. He did more research than that, of course, but the point is you can learn something by kicking the tires.

## COMPLETING THE PICTURE

Your hands-on research should complete the analysis you've already done. Good products and services are mandatory to a company's success. Of course, you don't always have to travel to do that. Use virtual bookstore Amazon.com, for example, and you'll understand some of the reasons for the explosive growth of the company's share prices, despite its complete lack of profits.

After you visit a company, send your tour guide a thank-you note. Expect a reply, by the way. How well a company treats its customers, the public, and its investors is a pretty good indication of how well it values these integral players in its ongoing success.

$$Chapter\ 16$$

# One Lean
# Investing Machine

In Chapter 1, we said the point of research is to find the information you need to carry out your investment strategy in the most effective, streamlined fashion possible. Since then, you've read here about the scores of advice and investment resources available to you, including annual reports, magazines, newspapers, newsletters, TV shows, and web sites. There are far too many for any one individual to keep up with or even monitor. So let's sort through our offerings and devise a base of resources that you can keep up with and monitor in a sane fashion.

But, while we've tried to give you every possible type of resource and offering, we can't tell you which ones you'll be comfortable with or use to your advantage. Whatever works for you is what works for you and we're not going to question it. Good investing is a little like painting a picture. Some artists paint people who look like people and make thousands. Other artists paint pictures of people who look like ice cubes. Whatever pays. Whatever works.

To build and maintain a portfolio in an ongoing fashion, however, you should have a subscription to at least one newspaper that has a decent investment section, so you can track your investments and get the news you need about the economy, markets, and companies. You should also take a look at a business or personal finance magazine on an ongoing basis, so you'll have a sense of some of the larger trends impacting investing. Such magazines are also good sources of a wide range of investment-related ideas, such as minimizing your capital gains tax bill, making sure your portfolio is on target, and checking for unnecessary fees.

Of course, those paper products are expendable if you go online most days. One or two web sites or news sites are probably all you need when it comes to getting your economic and market news and investment ideas and conducting your investment research. If you use an online broker, don't forget to take advantage of its news, market, and research capabilities as well.

## OUR WINNERS

Here's a look at our streamlined choices in the must-have categories.

### Select One Financial Newspaper

The *Wall Street Journal* and *Investor's Business Daily* both provide news, insight, and data on the markets. Both profile corporations and leaders. Each offers timely "news you can use" and consumer advice.

If you are a buy-and-hold investor who wants to stay abreast of the markets but make few stock or mutual fund transactions each year, the *Wall Street Journal* will satisfy much of your information needs. You get a discount on access to its web site if you are a newspaper subscriber. The web site includes a search service that makes available hundreds of thousands of articles from a range of publications.

If you find the action of trading stocks exciting and you see yourself making many trades in the course of a year, *Investor's Business Daily* will provide you with trend and market information aimed at aiding your decision making. Remember *IBD* is available online for free, at least for now, but focuses a good deal of its attention on technology.

## Choose One Financial Magazine

The ground around financial magazines is well plowed, so deciding among the *Worth*s and *SmartMoney*s is sometimes based as much on personal preference for the graphics as the content. This is particularly so now that *Money* magazine has restyled itself into a more reader-friendly, more practical investment publication. Still, there are differences, however small, that can influence your thinking.

SmartMoney has a sassy disrespect for the pontifications of stock analysts, and just about anyone else it takes a disliking to in its "Ten Things" column. *Worth* is pitched to an audience of higher net worth, as is *Bloomberg Personal*. We like *Money* and *SmartMoney*. But browse through a few copies at the library or in the bookstore before you make up your mind.

Of course, if you're a business manager, go with *Business Week*. There's too much business news for the average investor there, but if you need that information otherwise, *Business Week*'s mutual fund and investing advice is thorough and comes often enough in the magazine to make it a solid contender.

## Hankering for a Newsletter?

The *Hulbert Financial Digest* is *Reader's Digest* of investment newsletters since it tracks nearly all of the other recommendations newsletters make and rates their performance.

## The Best of the Web Sites

You can manage a portfolio from AOL's personal finance channel about as easily as you can from any site on the Internet. It has links to Motley Fool, Morningstar, and

Hoover's. Its business news comes from Reuters and the ABC network. Sage supplies much of its investment basics and First Call its analyst predictions on earnings growth. That's comprehensive enough for most investors, though you're likely to find yourself bookmarking many of these links so you can go directly to them. To go beyond AOL, here are our two favorite sites.

**Morningstar (www.morningstar.net).** If you own mutual funds, and you should, this is an all but one-stop source of information and data, insight and news. Be sure you bookmark the home page as "morningstar.net" not "morningstar.com" to get the most up-to-date fund performance.

**CBS MarketWatch (www.cbsmarketwatch.com).** This site is to stocks what Morningstar is to mutual funds. The link to a major network gives the news section an urgency that is sometimes missing from other web sites with thinner news-gathering resources.

### Building a Library

You'll get an excellent grounding in investing with the "Getting Started In" series published by John Wiley & Sons, of which this book is a part. The series has fundamental books that outline a variety of topics ranging from annuities to technical investing.

There are also several standard volumes on personal finance that include chapters on investing and are worth perusing, among them Jane Bryant Quinn's *Making the Most of Your Money* (Simon & Schuster, 1998). As an investor you'll probably want to develop a small, useful library of guides that provide the insights and parameters that can lead you to even more success. Call it collected wisdom. You've earned it.

**Beyond the Basics.** To give yourself a solid grounding in a variety of approaches to investing, sample some of these books to see which ones will work for you:

*Contrarian Investment Strategies*, by David Dreman (Simon & Schuster, 1998). A self- styled dean of contrarian investors, Dreman is president of Dreman Value Management LLC. It's based in Red Bank, New Jersey, but Dreman, perhaps to rub in just how successful his antiestablishment strategies have been, lives in Aspen, Colorado.

Dreman is a refreshing figure in an all too serious and egocentric gaggle of self-made millionaires who proffer their own theories of investment success as the one true way. With so many of them out there, it's obvious there are many routes to great fortune in the stock market. Dreman's contribution is to remind us that most foolproof investment plans are full of holes, as well as success. It's okay for you to believe in one of them as long as you remember it is only one strategy in a sea of strategies.

*Getting Started in Stocks*, by Alvin D. Hall (John Wiley & Sons, 1997). This book is a useful tool and reference guide for anyone who wants to pursue a long-term stock or stock mutual fund portfolio-building strategy. Hall, who is nicknamed the "Professor of Wall Street," packs this book with information on how to use stocks and mutual funds to diversify your portfolio, minimize risk, and exploit international opportunities.

*The Warren Buffett Way*, by Robert Hagstrom (John Wiley & Sons, 1995). With more than four decades of an unparalleled investment track record and $10 billion in personal wealth under his belt, Warren Buffett and his investment approach are worth examining and studying any day of the week. Hagstrom set out to identify and make Buffett's strategy understandable to even new investors and he has succeeded in his mission. Hagstrom himself is no chump. The Philadelphia money manager invests more than $10 million for clients, and also manages the Focus Trust mutual fund.

*What Works on Wall Street*, by James P. O'Shaughnessy (McGraw-Hill, 1997). O'Shaughnessy, an investment adviser in Connecticut, has done a statistical analysis of hundreds of stocks to determine which

**The Last Word on Investing**

• *Don't believe everything you read or hear.* From brokers who earn their living selling you investments to scam artists who would sell you the Eiffel Tower if you'd fork over some cash, there is no shortage of those who have a very vested interest in "giving" you "very valuable" information. Sound too promising? Too easy? Too good to be true? It is. We'll bet money on it. Keep in mind there really is no shortcut to successful investing or finding investment information that will bear fruit. You have to do enough homework, over a long enough period of time, to develop your own sixth sense about which investments will stay the course and work for you.

• *Don't feel you have to trade every day, month, or year.* Investment success, as you've heard so many times and will continue to hear if you keep building your knowledge, comes from refining an investment philosophy and staying the course. That strategy may be as simple as to find five decent mutual funds (large cap, small cap, mid-cap, bond, and international) and stick with them. Investors run into trouble when they believe they should sell at the drop of a hat. They miss out on the highs, but somehow always manage to experience the lows. Plus they have the additional drain on their performance of all the trading fees they incur.

• *Invest for the long haul.* Over the long term, stocks have historically outperformed all other investments, with a 12% average annual return—and that's since 1926. The next best performing asset class, which is bonds, returned just 5.2%. But over the short term, if you buy and sell often enough, stocks can play havoc with your financial picture. When the Dow Jones Industrial Average plummeted more than 550 points on October 19, 1987, it drained more than 22% out of the value of stocks in less than a day. Not the day you would have wanted to cash out short-term investments.

• *Don't override your own best judgment.* This really is our last—but we think very important—word on the subject of investing. If all signs point to go, but you have some niggling sense that your money would be better off elsewhere, dig in your heels and keep doing your homework. That next great mutual fund or stock may be just around the corner.

strategies deliver the greatest return—an obvious but excellent idea. What makes the book worthwhile is not that he arrives at a single strap-yourself-in-for-the-rough-but-millionaire-making-ride type of strategy, but several sane and safe strategies that have made lots of money for lots of people. The book sheds much light on the leading investment strategies. For instance, O'Shaughnessy's first rule of investing is that you must have a strategy. And you have to stick to it. He insists that a strategy, any accepted strategy, works only when it is applied consistently.

*A Random Walk Down Wall Street*, by Burton G. Malkiel (W. W. Norton, 6th ed., 1996). In his best-selling investment guide, Burton Malkiel maps a clear path through the dizzying array of strategies and products that pit the individual investor against the pros of Wall Street. It's a useful tool for personal money management. Malkiel is particular to long-term investing, which is a good strategy to underscore and elaborate on. He also looks at the seductive and potentially dangerous markets in futures and options. The book also includes an update of Malkiel's famous life cycle guide to investing, which will help you chart your penchant for risk and your aversion to risk.

*Stocks for the Long Run*, by Jeremy Siegel (McGraw-Hill, 1998). Siegel is a professor of finance at the Wharton School in Philadelphia. As the title implies, Siegel is a buy-and-hold investor. His book is a primer on investing that is among the most readable by an academic. Of value in understanding the book is Peter Bernstein's foreword in which he notes the real secret of investment success is knowing how to manage "the unexpected consequences of our decisions."

That might apply to more of our lives than just investing.

# Glossary

**active management** a style of mutual fund management in which managers continually select securities to buy and sell, as opposed to the passive style used in managing an index fund, in which the securities that make up an index are bought and held.

**aftermarket price** stock price created after the trading of shares in a company by the original buyers at an initial public offering. This price can be higher or lower than the IPO price.

**aggressive growth funds** funds that buy the stocks of new companies, small companies, and undervalued companies they expect to increase in value.

**annual expenses** the percentage of your investment that a mutual fund charges every year to cover its overhead and administrative charges including salaries.

**annual interest** the interest you earn in one year on an investment. On a bond, annual interest equals the coupon rate multiplied by the face value.

**annual reports** one of the chief communications tools for companies; should be viewed with some skepticism, as they are produced by the companies themselves.

**assets under management** the section of a mutual fund's prospectus telling you the fund's asset size, which is important in putting performance into context.

**B shares** a type of mutual fund that charges you annual fees.

**back-end loads** also called contingent-deferred sales loads, these are commissions that get passed on to brokers, which you pay when you sell your investment in certain mutual funds.

**balanced funds** funds whose portfolios are made up of about 60% stocks and 40% bonds.

**balance sheet** statement of what a company owns (assets) and what it owes (liabilities) at the end of the year.

221

**basis point** one-hundredth of a percent; a unit in which interest rates are measured.

**bond funds** funds that invest only in bonds, and may specialize in certain types of bonds based on the investment objective.

**book value** how much a company would be worth if it liquidated all of its assets and paid off all of its debt tomorrow.

**bottom-up investors** those who use a stock-picking strategy based on a search for value using fundamentals; tends to work best in a bear market.

**bull market** a market in which investments and prices are increasing, as opposed to a bear market, in which investments and prices are declining.

**business cycle** a regular and recurring cycle of accelerating business and profits within a sector, followed by that sector falling out of favor. The business cycle is a telling sign of where the country is economically—expansion, recovery, or recession.

**buy or sell order** an order you place either to buy or to sell bonds or shares of a stock.

**capitalization** the total value of issues of a company's stock; equals the number of shares outstanding multiplied by the price.

**cash flow** the amount of net cash generated by a business during a specific time, taking expenses such as depreciation into account.

**cash flow statement** shows the company's cash balances after the cost of business activities are deducted.

**compound interest** interest earned when you reinvest previously earned interest from your investments. By letting your earnings ride, you begin to earn interest on your interest.

**concentration** a lack of diversification in a collection of investments, which increases risk.

**coupon rate** the amount of interest that is paid to bondholders. The coupon rate can be fixed or floating.

**current ratio** the total current assets divided by current liabilities of a company. The ratio should be at least 1.

**current yield** the annual interest on a bond divided by its market value and multiplied by 100.

**day traders** those who buy financial instruments and then sell them in the course of a day, attempting to profit from minute market fluctuations.

**debt ratio** current liabilities, long-term debt, other liabilities, and deferred income taxes of a company, summed and divided by total assets. A reasonable debt ratio is considered to be 55 or under, although some companies can handle a higher ratio.

**derivative securities** any financial security whose value to the investor is dependent on some other security's value and characteristics. Examples are options and futures.

**discount** the amount below its face value that a bond is selling at.

**diversification** a strategy of spreading your money out in an array of investments, which ideally move out-of-step with each other, in an attempt to protect your overall portfolio against a potential loss in any one investment.

**dividends** the portion of a company's profits paid out directly to its shareholders. A company's board of directors decides whether a company will declare and pay a dividend, and, if so, how large it will be.

**Dow Jones Industrial Average** a well-known index made up of 30 large-cap stocks, which tends to be a psychological indicator, rather than a true measure of the stock market's performance as a whole.

**downside risk** the risk of losing your principal investment, proportionate to any rewards or performance gains you're likely to get in exchange for those risks.

**earnings expectations** an estimate of a company's earnings. Falling short of these estimates or exceeding them can greatly influence the price of the company's stock.

**earnings per share (EPS)** net profits of a company during a specified time period, divided by the number of outstanding common shares during that period.

**equity income funds** funds that seek dividend income and slightly more growth than growth and income funds. Their underlying investments are blue-chip stocks, with some utilities for dividends.

**federal deposit insurance** insurance a bank issuing debt buys from the federal government to protect investors against loss. Federally insured investments are safer than others, but generally pay a lower rate. Bonds are not backed by this insurance.

**financial highlights** a section of a mutual fund's prospectus providing you with net asset value, total returns, and total assets, as well as performance.

**flow ratio** a company's current assets minus cash, divided by current liabilities. Flow ratios of less than 1% are considered good.

**front-end load sales** a type of mutual fund that deducts its fees from your initial investment.

**fundamental analysis** a method of stock analysis that focuses on past measures—such as a company's earnings, market share, or sales—to estimate what will happen to the price of that stock in the future.

**fundamentals** the underlying, historical information on dividends, earnings, sales, and profits that can help you form a picture of a company's prospect for future success.

**futures** contracts to buy or sell a set number of shares of a specific stock or a set amount of some commodity at a future date and price. The contracts themselves are traded on futures markets.

**GARP** growth at a reasonable price—a type of analysis tempering growth investing with price parameters.

**growth funds** funds that own mostly big or medium-sized companies that look for long-term gain.

**hedge** to buy an investment that moves out-of-step with the rest of your portfolio, in order to diversify.

**hedge fund** a fund that may use many complex techniques based on valuation models to enhance its return, such as both buying and borrowing shares of a stock.

**income funds** funds that invest primarily in bonds and dividend-paying stocks.

**income statement** section of a financial statement that shows whether a company's operations turned a profit or generated a loss during the year.

**income stocks** stocks that offer higher dividends rather than higher earnings growth rates, such as utility companies.

**independent auditor's statement** a section of an annual report in which an outside person who audited the report states an opinion; must be included by all publicly traded companies.

**index** an average; a gauge of a particular market based on the computation of the average prices or price movement of a group of like investments.

**index funds** funds that invest in the stocks that make up a particular index. Their performance mirrors that of the overall market.

**inflation** the rate at which prices on goods and services will increase each year, reducing the purchasing power of today's dollar in the future.

**insider trading** the buying or selling of a company's stock by senior executives or major shareholders; seen as a signal that prices will change.

**interest income** the interest your investments earn in any given year.

**international, world, and global funds** funds that invest in a portfolio of non-U.S. stocks and/or bonds. They may also, in the case of world and global funds, invest in the U.S. markets as well.

**Internet browser** a software program that you use to access sites on the Internet.

**inverse correlation** a relationship between two measures in which an increase in the first tends to coincide with a decrease in the second. Bond prices and interest rates are inversely correlated.

**investment clubs** groups of about 15 members chipping in to buy a portfolio of stocks, and meeting monthly to review portfolios, report on analysis, and make investment decisions.

**investment strategy** a plan for investing that meets criteria such as your goals, time horizon, and tolerance for risk.

**investor confidence** the level of assurance being exhibited by investors, which can influence price movements.

**investor relations department** a department in a company you can call to obtain annual reports, quarterly reports, and company updates.

**junk bonds** debt issued by those in some danger of defaulting on their debt repayments. Owning junk bonds can therefore be very risky.

**leveraged** having a large proportion of debt as opposed to capital.

**limit orders** an order for stock that tells the broker you will buy if the price of the stock is below a limit you set.

**liquidity** a measure of whether a ready and willing market for the investment you want to buy or sell exists.

**loads** fees charged to you when you invest in a mutual fund.

**low-cost Internet provider service** a connection to the Internet that is cheaper than one of the large portals, but provides less guidance; good for when you've become more experienced with the Internet.

**market orders** an order for stock that tells the broker you will buy at whatever price the market is paying.

**market value** the last sale price multiplied by total shares outstanding of a company's stock.

**market-weighted** a type of index in which each stock in the index is weighted by its number of outstanding shares, thereby preventing skewed performance.

**maximum initial sales charges, commissions, or loads** fees you pay to have a mutual fund sold to you. They can range as high as 5.75%.

**medium company growth funds** funds that specialize in medium-sized companies whose market capitalization is under $5 billion. Also called mid-cap funds.

**mortgage-backed bonds** bonds issued by three government-sponsored entities, the Government National Mortgage Association, the Federal National Mortgage Association, and the Federal Home Loan Mortgage Corporation (Ginnie Maes, Fannie Maes, and Freddie Macs, respectively). They are backed by pools of mortgages that the associations buy, package, and sell on the secondary market.

**mutual fund indicators** the amount of money in mutual fund portfolios held in cash. Can be seen as an indicator of future big stock purchases (driving up prices), or stagnancy, letting prices decrease.

**mutual fund objective** the stated investment objective of the mutual fund manager selecting the fund portfolio. The three most common objectives are: growth, income, or both growth and income.

**Nasdaq Composite Index** the index that measures the market value of all common stock listed on the Nasdaq Stock Market; highly concentrated in high-tech companies.

**net asset value (NAV)** the price per share of an open-end mutual fund.

**net change** the difference between an investment's price yesterday and today.

**net profits** the profits of a company after taxes, preferred shareholders, and bondholders are paid.

**notes to financials** a section of an annual report that tells you about any changes in accounting practices of the company; also includes notes on litigation and so forth.

**offering price** the price of a stock when it is first publicly offered in an IPO. This price can increase or decrease within minutes of the initial trade if it is traded again.

**one-, three-, and five-year annualized returns** a measure of the earnings of a fund over the past one, three, or five years, which gives you an idea of how performance has held up over time.

**options** the rights to either buy or sell a set number of shares of a stock at a specified price within a specified amount of time—even if the market price of that stock is less or more than the price specified by the option. An option differs from a future in that you are not required to use the option to sell or buy.

**outstanding shares** the number of stock shares a company has issued and not bought back.

**over-the-counter market** a market for exchanging stocks in which the shares are bought over the counter at brokerage firms, as opposed to being listed on a stock exchange.

**performance** how much money an investment earns or loses in interest and dividends combined. Performance is a measure of how well, or poorly, your investment is doing.

**portals** servers providing usually unlimited access to the Internet through a phone or cable line, costing about $20 a month. Larger ones include AOL, MSN, and Infoseek, and often provide much financial information in an easy-to-find format.

**portfolio** a collection of investments owned by an individual investor or a company, including certificates of deposit, stocks, bonds, and mutual funds.

**portfolio turnover** the amount of buying and selling a mutual fund manager does, which affects both expenses and returns.

**price-earnings ratio (P/E)** the price of a stock divided by the company's earnings per share for the past year. This ratio is considered by some to indicate whether a stock is overvalued or undervalued.

**price-to-sales ratio** the price of a stock divided by its sales per share.

**price-weighted** a type of index in which stocks are not weighted by a company's size or number of outstanding shares. Unlike a market-weighted index, it overweights higher-priced stocks.

**principal** the amount of money you invest, on which interest is then earned.

**profit margin** net income divided by revenues. You can learn how well a company generates profits by comparing this number to those of the company's peers.

**projection** an estimate of how well an investment is likely to perform that is based on performance comparisons, analysis, and performance of the sector and economy as a whole.

**prospectus** a printed statement describing a fund that is distributed to prospective investors.

**quantitative analysis** a type of stock analysis relying solely on quantitative, mathematical methods of searching for opportunity.

**quarterly reports** reports companies distribute every three months to update information in the annual report; also called 10Qs.

**rating** a measure of how safe from default a bond is. Generally, a rating of A or above from such services as Moody's, Standard & Poor's, and Fitch's Investment Service is considered acceptable.

**risk** how much money a certain investment can lose. Risk is usually measured as a percentage of your investment. To give clients an idea of how much they may lose investing in stocks, many financial planners cite 30% as a level of risk.

**Russell 2000 index** the most widely used index for gauging the average performance of small-cap growth stocks; includes 2,000 stocks.

**S&P 500** the index that represents the benchmark against which most money managers gauge their performance. Nine out of 10 fund managers don't outperform this index in any given five-year period.

**S&P Global Index** an index that includes international stocks.

**S&P MidCap 400** an index measuring performance of 400 mid-cap stocks.

**S&P SmallCap 600** an index measuring performance of 600 small-cap stocks.

**screening** a search method that allows you to set parameters you want to satisfy in an investment, and then filters out investments that don't meet your criteria.

**search engines** these are tools of the Internet which allow you to, by typing in a word or phrase, retrieve all of the web sites that offer the information you're looking for and then some.

**sector funds** mutual funds that specialize in a sector of the economy. For example, the stocks of banks, insurance companies, and brokerage firms would make up the portfolio of a financial services sector fund.

**shareholder equity** assets minus liabilities of a company—what all investors put together own.

**shareholders** investors who buy shares when a company issues stock or ownership shares that it sells in the open or public market.

**shareholder services** the section of a mutual fund's prospectus that details the minimum investment, methods of withdrawal requiring written permission, and so forth.

**small company growth funds** funds that specialize in small companies whose market capitalization is under $1 billion. Also called small-cap funds.

**spam** anonymous e-mail you may receive, often touting stocks and other investments. You should probably ignore and delete such e-mail.

**standard deviation** how much an investment goes up and down in price in a fixed time period; a numeric measure of volatility. Higher standard deviation represents higher volatility or risk.

**style drift** a change in the investment style of a mutual fund manager, causing the investments in the fund's portfolio to work against the fund's objective.

**technical analysis** a type of stock analysis that tries to use patterns in investment prices to make decisions about when to buy and sell a stock; does not use fundamentals.

**ticker symbol** the abbreviation used to represent a company's stock in its listing on the appropriate stock exchange.

**top-down investors** those who use a stock-picking strategy based on selection of growing and high growth potential stocks within sectors that are generally doing well; tends to work best in a bull market.

**total return** a measure of a fund's total return to the investor, taking charges, dividends, and earnings into account.

**unit investment trust** a collection of stocks which, unlike a mutual fund, is listed on a stock exchange where you can buy and sell shares in it. The portfolio is mostly fixed.

**value funds** funds that look for bargain, or underpriced, stocks that fund managers believe will rise in the future.

**variable annuities** annuities from which the investor receives a periodic amount of earnings linked to the performance of a portfolio of investments underlying the annuity.

**volatility** how much an investment is likely to fluctuate (increase and decrease) in value. Volatility is based on historical ups and downs, as well as how similar investments have performed.

**volume**  the total number of shares traded on an exchange in a given period. Believed by some to indicate whether prices will go up or down.

**watch list**  a list of investments that you find interesting enough to monitor their day-to-day performance.

**year-to-date return**  how much a fund has earned so far this year.

**yield to maturity**  a bond's total return.

# Index

Wealth creation, 5
Webcrawler (www.webcrawler.com), 193
*What Works on Wall Street*
  (O'Shaughnessy), 217, 219
Wilshire 5000, 46, 111–112
Wilshire 4500, 112
Wilshire Small Company Growth, 112
Wilshire Small Company Value, 112
World funds, 41, 60
*Worth*, 12, 140, 215
*Worth* Online (www.worth.com), 140–141

Yahoo! (www.yahoo.com), 94, 109, 113,
  191–193
Yahoo! Finance
  (www.yahoo!finance.com),
  199
Year-to-date return, 86
Yield, bond, 64
Yield to maturity, 97

Zacks Investment Research, 129